A Journey to Point Omega

Josef Pieper Books Published by St. Augustine's Press

A Journey to Point Omega

Autobiography from 1964

Josef Pieper

Translated by Dan Farrelly

ST. AUGUSTINE'S PRESS

South Bend, Indiana

Manufactured in the United States of America.

1 2 3 4 5 6   25 24 23 22 21 20 19

Library of Congress Control Number: 2019955217

∞ The paper used in this publication meets the minimum requirements of the American National Standard for Information Sciences - Permanence of Paper for Printed Materials, ANSI Z39.48-1984.

St. Augustine's Press
www.staugustine.net

Contents

Where Does the Beam of Light End?

On this occasion I did not follow the rule of only writing the foreword when the book is finished. The title of the third and probably last volume of my autobiography was already fixed. However, the meaning, during the process of my writing the book, had unexpectedly changed, so that the introduction I had written some years previously (1980) needed a new formulation.

At first sight the title might seem arbitrary and deliberately "poetic." But in fact originally it was intended as something sober and precise. In any case, it is, strictly speaking, a quotation. It comes from my son Thomas when he was not quite eleven years old. At school he had learned how a "distance," which goes from point A to point B, is different from a "beam" [of light], which while it has a point a has no fixed point b.

In the first years after the war, each evening I would either tell my children a story or read them one. But when, during the story, for some reason or other an interruption was necessary, Thomas insisted that to make up for it the next story would have to be much longer than usual, a story like a "beam of light."

And so the title of the book was meant to express, first of all, that the depiction of events —probably not coming to light until after my death — would necessarily remain incomplete. But when I was writing the last chapter it became clear to me that the beam of lived life was not limited by a "point b" but would come to its end at what someone has called the "Omega Point" — which remains for us, as long as we live, an unfathomable mystery.

September 1987

I
Remembrance of the Dead and a Pilgrimage

"This beaming Thomas!" This or something similar was written about him in many of the countless letters which began to flood into the house after the sudden death of our eldest son. Particularly the new friends whom he had only recently made in America extolled the young man who was "always happy" and who charmed them, particularly by means of his magic tricks. And indeed he really was amazingly good at magic; I myself was never able to see through any of his tricks. The landlady in Berkeley, clearly a straightforward woman with a sound knowledge of people, spoke about the "happiest boy" she had ever met. Dan O'Connor, who had been in and out of our house for years when a student in Münster and had been friends with us for a long time, had in the meantime advanced to becoming a lecturer in philosophy at a college in the east of the U.S. and had kindly taken the new arrival for a week into his young family home when Thomas was en route to California. Even he ended a long letter with the assurance that one thing that would remain in their memory about Thomas was "his laugh, which stretched from one ear to another."

Had Thomas himself been able to read this praise of his happy, cheerful temperament, he would have been very surprised. At any rate, inside, his life looked completely different. The diary of the last ten months reveals a person both plagued by many fears and deeply worried, who writes down the lament: "Why do I have it so hard, Lord?" Hidden beneath the seemingly carefree happiness a darker inner fate was taking shape. And still in the "beaming" there was no hint of stress. The assumption of a friend — with a somewhat deeper insight — that Thomas purposely hid his true self under the mask of a problem-free, cheerful outer exterior is completely wrong. And so in what way joys and sorrows were connected in the soul of this son remains a puzzle which cannot be solved.

These were the thoughts that were going through our minds when, in the quiet of the morning in a secluded corner of a park, we were trying to decipher the notes which Thomas had left behind. My wife found it almost unseemly in that early autumn of 1964 to be travelling to the sunny south "for enjoyment" less than two months after the burial. But of course the flights and accommodation had been fully booked long in advance. It turned out that this opportunity for undisturbed self-reflection was very beneficial and really necessary. Awakened and removed from the numbness — but also from the turmoil of being so directly affected — we had a chance to look back calmly at what had happened. Of course we knew immediately that the completely unexpected death of our son and brother would utterly change our whole lives, and we were to say this to one another often enough, particularly on the anniversaries. But for the first time during those morning hours we began to realize that this loss, which had struck us like a bolt of lightning out of a clear blue sky, was to bring us something other than pain.

Incidentally, the mention of a bolt of lightning evoked a very specific memory for me. Many years previously, during the university holidays, I was staying for a few days with my uncle, a priest, and was by chance completely alone in the house when lightning struck in the rectory garden. It was a very short bright flash, followed, not by thunder, but by an eerie silence. The news of Thomas's death struck me in the very same way. For a fraction of a second there was a triumphant bright sounding noise and then absolute silence. At the same time I had the feeling that it was the first time that anything so incomparable had ever happened to me before.

After a while, completely unexpectedly, although hardly perceptibly, that new dimension of life opened up which, through the experience of death, likewise seemed intended for us. One minute I just could not manage to sit at the sumptuously laid dinner table without thinking of the banquet of eternal life. Also the wonderful words of the intercession for the dead which were later introduced into the canon of the mass will always seem as if recited from within my soul: "May we sit with them at your table in the kingdom of heaven as you promised!"

After twenty-eight years we looked back at our son's life which had ended, and we recalled to mind some of his personal characteristics. Besides, I had brought with me the family chronicle which I had been writing for the previous eighteen months. The last entry which I had long forgotten and which I was now looking at again, was written on board the Dutch ship "Waterman" on which I had returned from Canada to Rotterdam in September 1952, fifteen years ago. And because I had decided to end the chronicle, I had tried to sketch the family picture of our three children at the time and had added to it a few of their wishes and also of their fears for the future. With some amazement I read that Thomas, who at that time was sixteen years old, was seriously intending to become a priest. Of course, it did not surprise us that he did not become one. Still, it has to be said that many times when I passed his room, I would hear him praying aloud and spontaneously until he was well into his student years. And his American diary appears to show that as a young adult he had not given up this habit of talking to God before going to sleep, although it was now more in the style of Job. "Music is his real passion": this was impossible to omit from any biographical profile; and from memory I had added this story: Thomas, while in his later years

3

in second-level education, once returned from a two-week trip with his class, stepped into the living room, and as there was a Chopin piano concerto playing on the radio he forgot to say hello to us, threw himself onto the nearest chair and sighed spellbound: "At last music again!" In his last letter to me before his death, he wrote about a "Divertimento for string orchestra" by Béla Bartók which he had just heard, and he closed with a question about whether doing without such things was too high a price to pay "for his stay in America." When I reread the sentence in my attempted portrait of 1952 it made me think: "His strength is his susceptibility." It remained completely apt; but meantime we had experienced how much this "strength" was linked to the endearing weakness which later, in the death notice, I called "defenseless sensitivity for human demands." But there was still nothing seriously disturbing in this. And also the fear expressed at the time that perhaps our son lacked toughness, gumption, and strength of will was not confirmed. For example, before Thomas set off for America he had won his yellow belt in a judo group (of police officers!); he had, expressly as a test of courage, learned gliding and in a final examination earned his license to fly solo; besides, he had also meanwhile earned his life-saver badge, although it was not long since his younger brother, in a playful name-calling game in the style of cowboys and Indians stories, had called him with amazing aptness: "water-shy fish."

No, the disquieting part was hidden elsewhere and much deeper. It became apparent very early, and you had to go back many pages in the chronical to find it. And when I read a particular entry from long ago, the frightening remark of the ten-year-old boy stood clearly before my soul. During a walk with me Thomas stopped suddenly and said that he now knew what he wanted most. It was not long before Christmas, and I thought that he had suddenly thought of a special present; naturally children spoke like this continually during these weeks. I looked at him inquisitively — and then got the completely serious and clearly long-considered reply: "I would really like never to have been born." I do not remember anymore what I said to him; maybe words failed me. Thomas himself had never again said anything like that. And when at Christmas he had found his presents which I had carefully hidden — among them an alto recorder — he announced loudly through the house that he was "blissfully happy." My evening storytelling continued undisturbed as well as the puzzles and guessing games at the table (what's the difference between a jug and a pot, a thorn and a spike, a stem and a stalk?). We had a lot of joy from the quick, vigorous intelligence which Thomas showed in these games. Once he himself asked his five-year-old brother what the opposite of "pretty" was, to which the prompt and confident answer came: "vain." Not bad, I thought; and when Thomas met this wisdom with uproarious laughter I wanted to teach him a lesson and asked him the question what the opposite of a birch tree would be. "There is no such thing!" — "And why not?" Now you could actually see how things were beginning to function in the now eleven-year-old Thomas's head: the statement came which I still find amazing today: "Only intangible things can have an opposite!"

With regard to telling stories, it was my turn in the evening; but at table and when we were out with the children they also had their turn. Usually three words were given (for example: bell, bird, star) and a dramatic event had to be concocted as quickly as possible, using these words. Thomas was in his element with this. Without hesitation he would begin, full of imagination, to tell his story. On one occasion he managed to conclude with rhymes. He only noticed it when he had finished. It was a triumph. He could remember poems effortlessly if he liked them, and so the eight-year-old would suddenly say simple verses from Rilke's book of fairy tales, and then, later, poems and also Latin hymns. During a walk through the fields Thomas spontaneously told me once one of Svensson's stories, but in such a way that you would think he, and not the Icelander Nonni, had experienced it.

5

But this completely relaxed way of telling stories came to an abrupt end. By contrast with his younger brother, Thomas had little luck with his teachers, and one of them, with school-masterly pedantry, even managed to dry up entirely the flow of the boy's fantasy. I saw him sitting with his essay book, close to tears; he couldn't find the right words. "Write whatever you like!" "No, I am not allowed to."

But from now on not only was the invention of stories finished. Other worrying things which were there earlier now came to light again. In the most ordinary everyday things a frightening lack of inner stability, deeply upsetting also for him, would appear. One day he said he was no longer able to pray because he was not able to say every word with proper devotion. He was unable to give a clear answer to simple, factual questions. "So, how was school today? Were you given a Latin exercise?"— "I think so." If I pushed for a yes or no answer he would almost dissolve into tears. But, on the whole, such things did not dictate the course of our lives, and Thomas himself seemed only occasionally to be depressed by them. But his inner insecurity remained. In the summer of 1957, when I was setting off with my friend Schranz on the journey to Greece, Thomas — even though he had six semesters of study behind him — said, half in jest, but also half seriously: "Inquire of the oracle in Delphi what is to become of me." But the daily round of work in study, in the house, and in the garden went on as usual. Feasts were celebrated in the normal way; in the holidays we undertook bike-rides together, in twos or threes, throughout Germany and also in Italy, Flanders, and France. Above all, music-making, always resounding with passion and inspiration, clearly remained for Thomas a sphere completely untouched by any other problems. But I was sometimes surprised and somewhat troubled to see that he had a special love for Jan Pieters Sweelinck's variations on the song "My young life is at its end." But precisely in the coming years in which his fundamental insecurity manifested itself with such devastating vehemence that we thought he needed to be treated by a psychotherapist — precisely at this critical time music proved to be a refuge to which he could always flee and feel safe.

With regard to psychotherapy, I found — as someone necessarily looking in from the outside — confirmation of what I already knew "theoretically." I now became convinced that someone who has such direct access to the methodically exposed central core of another person must himself be "right" in his thinking about the fundamentals of our existence, and even be "right" in himself, if incurable damage is to be avoided. But in this case I was not simply an observer. I was involved. Before the treatment began it was carefully explained to me that the son's relationship with the father, which was very close, and perhaps even too close, would probably be dissolved and possibly turn into antagonism. I was prepared for this, and also willing to accept it. But I could not see why this change should be deliberately brought about and, through arbitrary misinterpretation of "early childhood experiences," should lead not only to his complete alienation but even to his opposition to me, his father, and to all I stood for. This was painful for my son and probably disturbed him even further. According to a cousin and friend, Thomas had admitted during a long "conversation on religion" after the Christmas midnight Mass in San Francisco — a good six months before his death — that he had to go to the other end of the world from his father in order to be of one mind with him again. And so I ask myself whether this return, which was to be a much deeper return than that to his father — as we later found out — is to be explained more by the geographical distance than by the psychotherapy.

Furthermore, in a completely unexpected way, the power of memory appeared in another form. Thomas had burnt the candle at both ends. For months he had worked almost every day without interruption at an electron microscope, had slept too little, and for

7

"recreation" at the weekends had driven his car several thousand kilometers around the country, so that one day, in his exhaustion, he was sent by his doctor into hospital and told to stay in bed for a week. In this enforced period of rest, something he had never thought about came to him: the thought of his own death, which, as neither he nor anyone else would have expected, was only two months away. When his cousin, full of concern, asked how he was, she was probably surprised to hear that this was a good opportunity to "take stock." In the little notebook which he brought with him into the hospital there are some pensive words: "Sometimes to see something or a situation *sub specie mortis* or *sub specie aeternitatis* [from the angle of death or eternity]. Many things are then not so important or so bad." That is the first entry. And a few pages further on: "to encounter the foundation [of one's own being]. Why be afraid of it?" A few months later, at the time of the summer solstice, all of that seemed to be forgotten. Thomas wrote to us that he was celebrating his "best ever birthday: water-skiing under a clear blue sky." — And then, scarcely a month later, with two friends he began his first real holiday since arriving in America. In a letter written to me shortly before he started out, he wrote: "Three great weeks coming up." The letter soon arrived, but by that time Thomas was already several days dead. He was suddenly taken from this world — in the evening of a cloudless summer's day, spent, as his companions later reported, in almost exuberant hilarity, in what was very possibly the very moment in which he found himself in harmony with God, the world, and himself.

Amongst the letters – of which I have spoken all too briefly — from friends and acquaintances on the occasion of my son's death, there were naturally not a few which served not only as expressions of sympathy, but which we also found moving because of the image of our son expressed in various kinds of living memories. A friend with much experience in dealing with psychologically troubled people wrote that, in dealing with his patients, the thought often came to him that their illness was "a sort of vocation or office in which they, standing in for many, bore and atoned for our wounded nature and carried the burdens peculiar to our time. Every time I saw and spoke to Thomas I had the definite impression that in this 'service' he was an honest and true servant." — Two years later, almost to the day, when Thomas would have turned thirty, a letter came from my publisher friend Heinrich Wild "as a sign of his constant sympathy with this mysterious fate." He spoke of a seemingly happy temperament, very different from a much more serious and almost melancholy heart, but which was at the same time "the expression of such a perfect human attitude of openness that it revealed not only something exemplary but something which we all seek as the source of happiness — yet hardly ever find. When we do encounter it, especially in someone so much younger, it is inalienable and unforgettable."

In the spring of 1965 we set off on our pilgrimage to the Holy Land — with Thomas in our minds and in memory of him. Since the most important sites connected with the memory of Jesus were situated outside of the state of Israel in the then partitioned Jerusalem, we decided on going to Jordan. We accepted as a political oddity that thereby, as the travel agent told us, access to Israel would be absolutely impossible for us. It seemed strange and, for the time being, mysterious that it was necessary to present a baptism certificate as a requirement for a visa to enter Jordan. Our plan was to remain in Jerusalem for two weeks and then to holiday for a time in Lebanon, at the beach in Beirut.

It turned out quite different, in fact. It started already in Germany that our "Boeing 727," which had just come into service, made uncanny sounds which suggested technical damage, had to relinquish its planned altitude, and decrease its speed. The repair work at Munich airport lasted so long that in Rome we missed our connecting flight to Beirut and could only continue our journey on the following day. We did not regret spending the evening and the next morning walking around the city of Rome, seeing again the Via Giulia which was so familiar to us from our first journey to Italy in 1933, and also seeing the central nave of St Peter's Basilica, now transformed into a hall for the Vatican Council. Besides, we thought it quite meaningful to begin the last leg of the journey from the second last point, whose story began in the place we had set out for. And then, when to our surprise in Beirut we were again not in time to catch our flight to Jerusalem, we overnighted — at the expense of the airline — in one of the big hotels which, fifteen years later, we would again see in the horrifying war scenes in Lebanon reported on television. But then, at least, as we walked around the hotel area in the evening, this city offered sights of a very different kind. The all-pervasive atmosphere of amusements and nightclubs was such that we immediately decided not to spend our planned holiday weeks there; and on the same evening we canceled the hotel reservation which had already been made for us. We presumed we would find something else. We did not realize that this would land us exactly where everyone thought access would be denied to us.

First we arrived in what was then, as I have mentioned, the Jordanian part of the city of Jerusalem — the expressly "non-Jewish" part, which was more radically isolated from Israel than we would have thought possible. Our small travel book did include some information about the Israeli section of the city, but on a loose leaf which, for the sake of caution, could be kept separately. When, not so innocent as we pretended to be, we inquired about a return flight via Tel Aviv, we were told in a tone of well-acted astonishment, that they did not know of a city of that name. The official description of the Dome of the Rock which we visited on our first day made no mention of the fact that this was precisely the temple of the Jews in which Jesus used to teach, and the veil of which was torn from top to bottom when He died on the cross. But we did learn that in the mosque next to the temple the grandfather of the present Jordanian king Abdallah was murdered in 1951 because he wanted to make peace with Israel – just as, three years previously, the Swedish Count Bernadotte was killed by Jewish fanatics because he wanted to reconcile the Israelis with the Arabs.

Our hotel, near the Jaffa gate and situated right at the boundary wall to Israel, was managed by a Christian Arab whose lively gestures and spontaneity we found attractive. Every time we returned from a walk in the city we could tell from the deeply apologetic, compassionate and worried look on his face that the mail we were impatiently looking for had not yet arrived; and then, when it finally did arrive as we were having our midday meal, he brought it to us at our table, beaming with joy, and with great ceremony made a big sign of the cross. With this engaging man we were having a conversation one day, and almost in passing, about the text by Arnold J. Toynbee — dozens of copies were laid around in the hotel lobby — who spoke of the great injustice done to the Palestinian Arabs by Israel. Suddenly he invited us — but without my camera, which could endanger us — to climb onto the roof of his house; and then he pointed to five or six buildings which the Jewish state had "taken away" from his relatives and friends. Naturally we were not in a position to check the truth of his statements; but they were confirmed again and again. And we became uneasy with what had been our spontaneous prejudice in favor of Israel.

But, to my surprise, something else caused me concern — something that affected me much more deeply. Naturally I had never considered it a "spent" idea, as Rudolf Bultmann calls it, "that a pre-existent divine being appeared on earth as a man." But here I was inwardly confronted with this truth — which, in faith, I had always affirmed and never doubted in all its mysterious incredibility — as something which became a bodily historical event right at the place where I now stood. It simply took my breath away when I read in the Church of the Nativity in Jerusalem the words inscribed in the silver star: "Here Jesus Christ was born of the Virgin Mary." And for the first time the flame was ignited.

Until then this had not happened to us in Jerusalem. Only now did we become aware how much we had secretly wished for it. We had come back from the walk along the *via dolorosa* rather disappointed. Identifying individual stations of the cross, for example, as the chapel of Simon of Cyrene or the House of Veronica we found quite problematic. And the throngs of tourists and pilgrims made it impossible to have the listening silence which we thought necessary here. — The most depressing experience was our first visit to the Church of the Holy Sepulcher; we did not want to join the group led by a man speaking in a loud voice, with the result that we were not able to see very much. And when an Armenian monk beckoned to me to have me crawl into a dark hollow at the back of the sacred tomb — the "real" grave of Christ — and sprinkled a few drops of "holy water" on the back of my hand with a bulb syringe, and held out his other hand to receive a baksheesh, we were confused and saddened as we quickly left the Church we had visited with high expectations. But a short time later we would touchingly be given access to its sanctuaries.

But at first it seemed like flight when we set out in the cold winter's morning to go to the Crusader Church of St. Anne at the other end of the city. There, almost alone in the nave of the church, we attended a Mass celebrated in rapturous meditative calm by Melchitic White Fathers. Out in the open again, we paused to look down at the excavated remains of the columned hall of the Bethesda pond (about which individual historians of religion, as recently as thirty years ago, had assumed that the author of St John's Gospel had freely created it for symbolic purposes).

One day, someone gave us — I think it was our Arabic host in the hotel — two pieces of advice which we followed. We should go to a particular house and descend into the cellar, which, although accessible to everyone, was rarely visited. He said the house was built above a city gate. Just like the earlier defensive wall, it had been covered over with centuries of debris, but was now uncovered. The Church of the Holy Sepulcher, just one hundred meters away, which also overarches the hill of Golgotha, is in the middle of the densely populated modern Jerusalem; but now we understood what is said in the New Testament: namely, that Jesus "was led *out*" to a place near the city to be crucified and that "he suffered outside the gate." And looking at the stone threshold of the gate worn down by innumerable feet, hooves, and cart wheels, we were convinced that Jesus must have walked over it on his way to Golgotha. Then as with devout hearts we did the same, the gate, which until then had been closed, suddenly opened slightly for a moment.

Of course it did not open entirely until we followed the second piece of advice and visited the Sepulcher not in bright daylight but in the evening at dusk shortly before it was closed. The stream of visitors had ebbed away and we found ourselves, as in St. Anne's early in the morning, almost alone in the polynomial, vast space in the gathering darkness. Each time, we immediately climbed up the steps to the "Chapel of the Crucifixion" to what has been fairly unanimously confirmed by historians as the hill of Golgotha. Under one of the altars there is a spot visibly marked as the spot where the cross of Jesus Christ stood. At no time did we dare to touch it; but even so, what radiated from this place — with which nothing else in the world can compare — touched us with its overpowering force. In silence we knelt down and contemplated death — the one suffered here many centuries ago and the one that had been visited on our son and on us.

On the way back we were not inclined to speak to one another, and we were not embarrassed when, more or less surreptitiously, we used handkerchiefs to wipe tears from our eyes.

But since the real object of our journey had been achieved we were now able to take great pleasure in the incredible brilliance of the colors and — despite all the visible hardship — the cheerful noise in the narrow streets and bazars of the old city of Jerusalem. We watched the production of an ornament in the workshop of an Armenian silversmith; contemplated colored fabrics as we drank coffee presented to us on a brass tray; or, at the Damascus Gate, looked at the waves of people flooding in and out of the city. There was a young Arab who called himself "Lulu" — which according to him meant "pearl" — who soon considered himself to be "our" driver and stopped his taxi beside us as soon as we appeared. So we then drove with him to Hebron, to Jericho, to the Dead Sea, and even for a whole day to Damascus (which brought with it the expensive surprise of having, on the return journey, to request and to pay for a new visa for entry into Jordan). But now we were very anxious to see Nazareth, and Capernaum, and the Lake of Gennesaret. But that was all in Israel. And I was not prepared to think it impossible to go there. After all, my friend Leo von Rudloff was Abbot of the Benedictine monastery on Mount Sion, the Dormition Abbey. And how often had we not heard of the "Almond Tree Gate"! So I went one morning to the offices of the "Latin Patriarch," whom, of course, I was not able to reach personally; but his Vicar General asked to see my passport, listened as he scrutinized me and soon let me into the secret that "naturally" every day there were people with connections to the Benedictine Abbey and that any message from me would be answered no later than the next day. And in fact, only a short time later we had application forms and questionnaires to fill out; and again it was not long before "Lulu" brought us to the Almond Tree gate. But beforehand, as we departed from the hotel we had to put baksheesh into no less than sixteen hands. As we were on our way to the taxi another person, who did not belong there, joined the row of people and was laughed at gleefully by the others when he went away empty-handed.

Our somewhat romantic notions about the Almond Tree Gate

were very quickly corrected. There was neither a gate nor even an almond tree; instead, there was nothing more than a flattened area of rubble on which a large store had once stood which belonged to the Almond Tree [Mandelbaum] firm. It was an empty rectangle around thirty meters wide and seventy meters long. At one end was the customs house for Jordan and at the other for Israel. The Arab "Lulu" could only bring our luggage as far as the line drawn at the half-way mark, and that is where it remained, too, while in the Israeli custom house we dealt with the rather complicated entry procedure; seemingly, on this particular day we were the only ones making the crossing. At one point, when rather anxiously I looked out the window at our luggage standing out there in the open, an Israeli customs officer laughed. He was obviously originally from Berlin. "Your luggage is nowhere safer than where it is at the moment. If anyone touches it shots will be fired!" Through the glass door we had already seen a young Benedictine who was then let in and collected our luggage from no man's land. It was Brother David from the Dormition Abbey, a somewhat boyish American who had no word of German. When I remarked that we had survived the Almond Tree adventure, he said that the next adventure was immediately in front of us. "How do you mean?" "Well, we are going through the orthodox part of Jerusalem, and today is the Sabbath!" — "So?" — "If we are lucky we'll get through without trouble; but they might also stop us or throw stones at us." At first, we couldn't believe it. But then it was again and again proved to be the case. For example, we were told that if, on the Sabbath, an ambulance was to bring a sick person to hospital without hindrance it would always have to have a police escort. "Is it permitted to heal on the Sabbath?" And so Jesus's question is relevant today. — With curiosity and somewhat worried, we drove through the quarter inhabited by the strictly orthodox Jews; some seemed to look at us with disapproval, but nothing happened to us. But that orthodox Jews were forced to live in a ghetto in their own city of Jerusalem was incomprehensible to us. "But that is exactly how it is," said Brother David. I was reminded of the bitter words of the satirist Ephraim Kishon: "We, too, have our Jews!"

And so now, contrary to our expectations, we had come to Israel. The answer to the question we usually asked — what was "different" here — was somewhat disappointing. We found ourselves no longer in the Orient but in a typically European-American city; people on the street went single-mindedly about their business. No dashes of color or cheerful noise. It is true that no one stretched out a hand to receive baksheesh, but neither were we served a cup of coffee. Of course, another difference would only become clear to us when we left Jerusalem. On the Jordanian side our road led to Jericho through a stony wilderness, just as it did two thousand years ago; but in front of the gates of the Israeli city was rich grassland, watered and made fertile by Jews who had only recently arrived from all parts of the world.

And so our "pilgrimage to the Holy Land" suddenly came to an end — for a while, at least. The memorial sites normally shown to visitors in this part of the city scarcely corresponded to historical reality — neither the "Last Supper Room" nor the room in which Mary died, even though the Dormition Abbey is named after it. What we thought was more authentic was, if not the burial place of David, then at least the smoke-blacked niche in its exterior wall, which for the time being for Jewish believers took the place of the Wailing Wall which was no longer accessible to them and at which, as we were told, loud lamentations could be heard during the Passover Festival. We were rather unprepared for the confrontation with Judaism — manifesting a form reaching back to Old Testament times, alongside its present political reality. We were not familiar with either of the aspects, and sometimes we found them alienating. And there was no lack of questions we wanted to ask. Very quickly we were to find someone who would provide us with information to our heart's content. Since he sometimes repeated the same warning — which made us uncomfortable and which we had already heard from Brother David – not to mention his name in any reports we might make ("Don't quote me"), he is to remain anonymous here as well. On 21 March, a Sunday, and the feast of St. Benedict as well, our friend celebrated with his monks a Pontifical High Mass with such solemnity that it made us forget the bags of sand with which, as we came from outside, we saw the Abbey dome protected. Besides, since the seventy-year-old Prior of the cloister was celebrating his saint's day, there was a small reception at which wine from Tabgha was served, the strange history of which we would soon hear more about. At this very reception I was greeted, to my surprise, by an Israeli whom I would not have been thinking about and who had almost entirely slipped from my memory. Some years previously he had been a guest in our house for a few hours. He was a Jew converted to Catholicism who had thereby lost his public office. At the time he was on a trip around West Germany which was funded by the Bonn government. We now told him about our unexpected permission to cross the border and arranged to meet him in our hotel the next afternoon. It would, as we immediately prophesied, probably turn out to be a kind of interview. Our guest laughed in agreement. The meeting began with his apology for not being able to return the hospitality we had shown him in Münster. He was living with his wife, also a convert to Catholicism, in student lodgings. He could not afford anything better from the money he earned from Abbot Leo for translating the texts of the Mass into Hebrew. "But now question me to death!" And that was exactly what we did. We came to the point immediately. "And so an Israeli cannot become a Catholic?" "Yes, he can; but then he loses his job." "Let us suppose that one of the twenty employees in the big bank where I changed money a while ago becomes Catholic. What will happen to him? Why would anyone notice? His skull cap — at least he will not be wearing that anymore." "Well, it begins with the skull cap. Originally the orthodox Jew covered his head only in the synagogue or when he prayed; but now the religious symbol has been made into a nationalist symbol. It no longer means 'I am Jew who prays,' but I am an Israeli.' His conversion could easily be kept secret; but the Catholic priests take the directives of the Ministry for Religion more seriously than they need to, and they report, out of fear, every change of religion." "And then?" "The employee is not immediately sacked." "But?" "But a higher official in the Ministry for Religion will after a while telephone the director of the bank and ask him the inquisitorial question whether and how long he can expect his customers to be served by a non-Jew. And then one day the sacking will be inevitable." — "Can a Jewish man marry a non-Jew?" — "No, that is impossible even from a legal point of view. Concubinage is acceptable, at least for inheritance purposes. Those who have the money travel to Cyprus to get married to their Christian partner. The crazy thing is that, at the most, only twenty per cent of Israelis are orthodox Jews; the average educated person here is an agnostic who knows his bible." We asked him his explanation for the expropriation of Arabic houses. It is a very complicated thing; and his attempt to answer made the interview falter somewhat. In the first great warlike appropriation of land in 1947/48, which will remain the really problematic issue, the Israelis conquered almost the whole of Galilee and a part of the city of Jerusalem. Eighty to a hundred Arabs deserted their houses and a good part of their possessions and fled to the safety of what is today Jordan, Syria, and Lebanon. What Israel calls "flight" the Arabs call "forced displacement." At that time Israel recalled the fugitives but at the same time gave them a deadline: anyone who did not return by 1949 forfeited his right to property. Most of the refugees stayed away but for expressly political reasons were not integrated by neighboring states but settled in camps with a view to keeping hostility to Israel alive. That is the way it is seen from the Israeli point of view. We reflected on what we heard in the

Jordanian part of the city and suspected that it had to do with one of these issues about which the truth was simply not to be discovered, at least not yet. — But our interview was not yet at an end. We had bought ourselves a bright picture postcard to shock the Israel enthusiasts amongst our friends; it showed a company of uniformed marching girls armed with machine pistols. "These are all volunteers! Women can refuse to become soldiers." "But men cannot?" "No. You can declare yourself mentally ill; but who wants to do that? Or you will be locked up. But, no, there is another possibility, although only for a strictly orthodox Jew; and such a one is easy to identify: clothing, hair style, etc. If a young man insists that study of the Torah is more important to him than serving with arms he is not then exempt from service but is considered to be on 'study leave'."

We asked what the convert thought of orthodox Judaism and we then heard him speak with reserve, but also with respect, about men who spend their whole lives in a Talmud school in extreme poverty; he told us about an old woman who did not want to go abroad to visit her children for fear that the Messiah might come and she would not be there. Finally he told us about a group of Yemenite Jews who had waited for months for transport to Israel, and then on a Sabbath day, refused to bring their luggage to the plane that was collecting them; they had never seen an airplane up close, but they were convinced that airplanes were the "wings of the eagle" on which God, according to the Book of Exodus, would bring his people to Himself.

To our surprise, we found it was getting dark outside; we parted company with a kind of puzzled gratitude for this fascinating and, at the same time, confusing introduction to a world which — as we would soon see in a much more drastic way — was completely unknown to us.

The altitude of the city of Jerusalem is more than 750 meters, so that it is to be taken quite literally when in the Gospels it is

19

several times reported: "Jesus went *up* to Jerusalem." Even this piece of information in the travel guide had been quite a surprise for us. But it was an absolute surprise to learn that to reach the lake of Gennesaret and the towns around its shores we had to descend 200 meters *below* Mediterranean Sea level. But we were preparing to do exactly this when, after a few days after our arrival in Israel, we set out in pouring rain in the Dormition Abbey's Citroën en route for Tiberias. It was an unpleasant journey. The driver was Brother David, the youngest of us; next to him sat the Abbot, and inside the car the five of us tried to sort ourselves out somehow; on the roof of the car was the luggage, protected by a tarpaulin. Apart from Leo von Rudloff, my wife and I were the only Germans. Little was said, and then only in English. The abbot himself, although born in Germany, had by diverse routes become an American citizen. Shortly before the outbreak of World War II, much to his chagrin he had been sent to the United States to check out the possibilities of some kind of settlement for his brethren who had been expelled from their Westphalian monastery Gerleve by the National Socialists. But then the war came and kept him in America. He established a priory in the state of Vermont and in 1945 returned to his monastery at home. But now, since the Dormition Abbey, built on Mount Sion by the German Kaiser Wilhelm II, was entrusted to the Beuron Benedictines — German monks, among whom were also the Gerleve monks; and since, on the other hand, after all that had happened in Germany the Israeli Jews could hardly be expected to accept a German abbot, the "American" Leo von Rudloff — who, by the way, had removed the "von" from his name while he was in the United States — seemed the right man for the position. He also introduced into the Dormition Abbey some of his monks from Vermont.

On the way, Brother David pointed out to us some interesting things — for example, the grim building in which Eichmann's trial took place; the gallows where he had been executed; the tanks which had been abandoned on the side of the road in the 1947/48 war. We took a midday break in the noisy self-service restaurant of a bus station, which could easily have been in Wisconsin or Ohio. Finally we alighted in Tiberias at the hotel which had been booked for us. The Abbot wanted to drive on to Tabgha, a small monastery belonging to the Dormition Abbey. The rain had stopped, there was a clear sky, and Brother David removed the tarpaulin and took down our luggage for us. I asked him the meaning of the Hebrew word on the bronze plate beside the hotel entrance, to which he replied conspiratorially: "That means 'Kosher'." From the balcony of our room we looked down in disbelief on the lake of Gennesaret lit up by the evening sun. We were not yet able to believe we were here. At the restaurant we were welcomed by the manager of the hotel who spoke German with a slight Berlin intonation. His welcome was particularly friendly precisely because we were his only non-Jewish guests. But the very next evening there were problems arising from this.

A glorious spring day had just ended. In the morning I had sat on the sunny balcony above the lake and begun to write down the text for a lecture I had agreed to give at the next meeting of our ecumenical work group. The theme was: "What is meant by 'God speaks'?" To my left, not far away, was the village Magdala, from which Mary Magdalen came. Further on, only just visible in the early morning mist, was Capernaum. A little further to the right, the Golan heights from which, shortly before midday, artillery fire could be heard, which, as we were assured, was only a Syrian demonstration and was of no significance. Opposite me on the shore at the other side of the lake, Bethsaida must have been — the home of the apostle Peter and his brother Andrew, and possibly also of John and James, the sons of Zebedee. In the afternoon I sauntered through the town and looked attentively at the mosque, which was visibly falling into ruin, and finally, following a signpost I arrived at the grave of Moses Maimonides. When I entered the spacious circle which was surrounded by a wall, the custodian of the grave rushed out with his arms held aloft in warning, with a skullcap made of stiff cardboard in his hand. I took my beret from my pocket and now, without further hindrance, approached the mound of the grave which was whitened with chalk, under which, according to the (as I later found out, problematic) tradition, the mortal remains of the Jewish philosopher I highly respected were thought to rest. The custodian asked me if he should say a prayer on my behalf; when I said yes, he wanted to know my name, and then he took hold of my arm and put his other hand on the grave and began to recite a rather lengthy Hebrew prayer, in which I frequently heard the word "Pipper" recurring. Entering the town of Tiberias used to be not permissible for a Jew — because the Roman occupying forces had built it over a cemetery. Jesus also seems to have avoided it. Yet the single verse of John's gospel that mentions the name Tiberias indicates that the miraculous feeding of the five thousand must have taken place near this very town.

Mulling over all these things I arrived back at the hotel just in time for the evening meal. Pleasantly tired and rather hungry, I sat down to table with my wife. The excellent wine, which took its name from Mount Carmel and probably also came from there, let my thoughts wander over the many historical developments which had originated from this part of the world. But then we found ourselves drastically, with a stroke, brought back to the here and now. The otherwise lavish menu offered as a dessert only sweet things and canned fruit; I would have preferred a few slices of cheese to go with the wine, and so I asked the waiter to bring me some. But with this, as I thought, completely simple request I had, without suspecting it, started a real avalanche of totally incomprehensible dissension. The waiter seemed extremely shocked and took a step back. "Sorry, we have no cheese." — "But this morning at breakfast there were half a dozen different kinds of cheese!?" But the waiter, a friendly man and already a little acquainted with

us, produced another bare "Sorry" and went off. We were still wondering about this when the deputy manager came and discreetly
asked us to understand that for religious reasons cheese could not
be served. We looked at her uncomprehendingly, but then she too
went without saying another word. I began to suspect that this had
something to do with the bronze plate at the entrance to the hotel,
and I thought of the face Brother David made, as much as to say:
you'll soon see! After a while the deputy manager returned to our
table to tell us that she had telephoned the management and that
it was after all possible to bring us the cheese to go with our wine.
I assured her that of course we respected their religious reasons
and asked for a fruit salad to be brought instead. But that was by
no means the end of the story. At breakfast the following morning
the manager appeared at our table, in his good humor rubbing his
hands: "This evening you will have cheese for your dessert; no
problem at all." Nothing had to be done except to change the table
cloth and bring other plates and other cutlery. "And then, of
course, you will be served cheese." But we insisted that we did not
want any special treatment but that we would like to know about
the "religious reasons." But this man of the world was not able to
tell us anything; all he could tell us was the fact that, according to
Jewish law, all food that had anything to do with milk was to be
kept completely separate from meat dishes of every kind — so
much so that not only different crockery and cutlery were to be
used, but that these also had to be washed in different basins. "And
what would have happened if yesterday, without fuss, we had been
served cheese?" Our manager made an imploring gesture which
was not altogether in tune with his ironically dismissive way of
speaking! "We are a kind of 'theocracy'! You have, of course, seen
the plate outside with the word 'kosher'? That means that we are
constantly under rabbinical scrutiny!" — "But in Jerusalem there
are restaurants without this sign!?" — "Yes, Jerusalem is a big city;
here in Tiberias we cannot take such liberty; we would lose our

license, which is very important for us." But now I wanted exact information and asked: "What, for example, would you lose?" — "For example, the right to cater for wedding parties; and that is the biggest part of our business."

And so, when our manager turned to go, it was not a little that we had learned. But he came back again to tell us that tomorrow evening was the beginning of the Sabbath and it would perhaps be better if we came into the dining room a little later. We, too, had this time thought of the Sabbath; but now there was something further to learn. We read in the weekly calendar of events *This Week in Israel* that in Jerusalem the Sabbath began on Friday at 17.11, in Haifa at 17.21, and in Tel Aviv only at 17.29. Tiberias was not even mentioned.

At midday that same day, our second in Tiberias, Brother David appeared in a somewhat touristically modified monastic habit to drive us around the countryside a while and finally to Tabgha. This happened almost daily from now on — for a whole week. And so we did come to see something of this hilly Galilee — gloriously decorated with bright spring flowers — which as the historians say, used to be unbelievably densely populated. Our friendly driver obviously intended first of all to give us a major surprise; he suggested driving to Chorazim, and naturally we agreed. Suddenly he stopped: "So, that is Chorazim!" We saw all around us nothing but land covered with high grass and wild flowers. "Where is Chorazim?" He laughed. "Walk around in the grass a bit!" And indeed we then saw, under the green grass, carved stumps of pillars and capitals. We looked at Brother David in astonishment and disbelief. "Yes, that is what is left of the town of Chorazim; Jesus cursed it!" Silently we climbed back into the car, which Brother David had in the meantime turned around. "We had better not drive any further; we could easily come under fire from the Golan Heights." And so it was not just a harmless Syrian demonstration. As if it was natural and planned, we drove "home" to Tabgha, whose name, as we had already been told in Jerusalem, was an Arabic corruption of the Greek word "heptapegon" [seven springs]. Tabgha is a place worthy of special veneration. In the once very simple church built of wooden beams and also called the "Church of the Multiplication of the Loaves," one can see beneath the altar the famous Byzantine floor mosaics showing the basket with five loaves and two fishes beside them. When we arrived there, a choral service immediately began, celebrated in the afternoons by the abbot and four or five of his monks and which we attended each day until we left for home. No one knew yet that almost ten years later, in Vermont in America, deeply disappointed with a totally different kind of Mass service, I would remind the abbot, in an intense debate which was not without bitterness, of these incomparable hours in Tabgha. For us, those late afternoons in the church at the lake of Gennesaret were similar to the experience we had during the evening visits to the Church of the Holy Sepulcher in Jerusalem; the stream of visitors had dried up and we were almost alone with the monks. And unexpectedly we were overjoyed to realize that something we had in the meantime forgotten about was restored to us, resumed, and from now on renewed every day: our pilgrimage to the Holy Land!

The next afternoon was entirely reserved for a visit to Tabgha. The actual head of the house, a Yugoslavian monk who did not like to be addressed as "Prior," conducted the tour; with an ancient, long-bearded German lay-brother monk, he lived here for the most part alone. We spent a long time in the church in which large areas of mosaic floor had been uncovered; we walked around the neighboring land near the shore where tradition places not only the multiplication of the loaves but also the Sermon on the Mount and the appearance of the resurrected Lord. Naturally there is also talk about the obvious everyday worries. "What do you think we live from? Can you imagine that we live from wine?" We had already heard about this in Jerusalem. But a grapevine was nowhere to be seen. And now this inventive jack-of-all-trades, who had been an officer in the British Army in World War II, showed us his wine-press. At the door of an old shed the priest bent down to dig a key out of the sand and opened the shed. Naturally, apart from a few plastic containers and several shelves with bottles, there was not much to see. In answer to our question about how much wine was produced here he said, very much in passing: last autumn, up to about 15,000 liters. "And the vinicultural expert?" Again offhandedly: "That's me; you can learn that kind of thing very quickly from books. But I do have good helpers." As he spoke he pointed through the window at two small houses in which Christian Arabs lived with their families. At the same moment he slapped his forehead, quickly locked the door, buried the key and ran to the monastery. Turning around he called to us: "A moment! I must show you something and tell you a story." When he returned he showed us some photos of the visit of Paul VI a good year ago. One of the photos was of a rather turbulent scene; arms raised in defense, behind which two men in working clothes force a passage for themselves. "Those are my Arabs!" And now followed a hardly believable story. During the Pope's trip to Israel, restricted to two days and, according to the government's wishes, to be managed with as little sensation as possible, a fair number of guests of honor had arrived in Nazareth for the Mass celebrated by Paul VI. Among them were clerics and laymen, Catholics, Greek Orthodox, and even Jews. At the reception planned to follow the Mass it was suddenly noticed that the Pope, who had as yet had no breakfast, was nowhere to be found. He had innocently gotten into the waiting car, the Israeli driver of which, a silent man who clearly could not speak a foreign language, immediately followed the strict instructions of his superiors to bring the Pope as quickly as possible to the next place he was visiting. And that was Tabgha. The car also drove through Cana. But there was no one to say to the Pope: this is Cana! In

Nazareth a motor-bike rider was promptly sent to catch up with the Pope's car and to announce his arrival in Tabgha. And now the eyewitness account, less a report than dramatic theater: "They called out to me: 'The Pope will be here in a few minutes and he has to be served coffee!' — 'All right, but who is to receive the Pope if I have to go into the kitchen?' So I ran up to the Arabs: 'Hurry up and make some coffee — the best you have ever made — for the Pope, and then bring it as quickly as you can!' When I came back the Pope was just getting out of his car and asked: 'Where am I?' — 'Holy Father, welcome to Tabgha!' I kissed his ring and led him through the church to the altar. Thank God the candles were already lit. The Pope knelt down to pray. Meantime, several cars were stopping outside; a swarm of photographers and reporters was arriving; there was a glare of flashlights. A little late the Pope's entourage arrived. Then, in no way to be deterred, my two Arabs marched in. On the brass tray was a long-stemmed pot and a small cup. I poured the coffee, but it was boiling hot. The Pope could not drink it. 'Holy Father, that's the way we make it here. In a high arc I poured the coffee three or four times from the pot to the cup and back again. The Pope smiled and took a few sips. But he had hardly knelt down again on his prie-dieu when one of his entourage came and whispered something to him. The time allotted to Tabgha was up. We accompanied the Pope to his car. Somewhere else, I thought, there will be another reception."

When we returned to the hotel the ritual for the beginning of the Sabbath was still going on in the dining room. We remained standing at some distance from the wide-open door. The rabbi turned his back on us. All the male guests were wearing skullcaps. The waiters had put white folded serviettes on their heads. When, after the soup, some apparently American guests lit cigarettes, a waiter came immediately and said: "Please don't smoke. It is the Sabbath!" — We thought, naturally, that smoking was not proper on the Sabbath, just as one does not smoke while praying or in a church; and we found this quite understandable. But we did not know how wrong we were until our Benedictines enlightened us.

On *Laetare* Sunday Brother David collected us for the usual early morning drive. He said the Abbot was waiting with his monks to talk to us. But we wanted to visit Capernaum first. But this time we did not want another surprise. Naturally we were familiar with the biblical stories of the "centurion of Capernaum," the healing of the man whose hand was withered since childhood, as well as the daughter of Jairus — an official of the synagogue — whom Jesus brought back to life, calling her by the gentle name *Talitha*, which is always left untranslated ("little lamb"). At first we had no clear memory that this town, too, like Chorazim, was cursed, but even more vigorously; but we had read it again in Matthew's Gospel: "And as for you, Capernaum, did you want to be exalted as high as heaven? You shall be thrown down to hell. For if the miracles done in you had been done in Sodom, it would have been standing yet" (Matt 11, 23). And so, baffled and silent, we walked around the ruins of Capernaum, of which the New Testament says it was his town — that he was "at home" there.

Then in the monastery there was a reception. Despite it being the Lenten period there was a glass of Tabgha wine, for which the appropriate name seemed not yet to have been found. Naturally, we had more to ask about than to report. When we mentioned, in passing, being impressed by the ban on smoking during the Sabbath, they laughed and explained that it was not about smoking. "Then what?" "The match! A Jew is not allowed to light a fire on the Sabbath!" But then we wanted to know about this strange separation of milk and meat. We would never have guessed the answer. We were not thinking of the fact that in the Book of Exodus it says several times: "Thou shalt not cook a kid in his mother's milk!" But that the Talmud's interpretation of the "Law" sees precisely this text as the God-given absolute command requiring this separation — that was something beyond our comprehension. This brought up the whole theme of "theology" for discussion. When my definition that theology is nothing but the attempt at interpreting revelation was more or less accepted, I proposed for discussion the question of whether in contemporary Judaism there was any theology at all. "Does interpretation not mean translating into another language and contemporary way of thinking while retaining, of course, the identity of the "original text"? One person said that in Israel there is undoubtedly genuine piety and deep religiosity, but not theology in such a sense. The name Martin Buber was mentioned — at which another person commented that the Hebrew university accepted him only with considerable reservations and certainly not as a "theologian"; and Buber himself had criticized the state of Israel very strongly. His statement — not easy to interpret — was quoted: "If Israel wants less than what it is meant to be, it will fail to achieve this which is less." But, of course, the question remains: what is Israel meant to be? — We parted deep in thought and went together to celebrate High Mass and Sunday Vespers.

We had not thought of the fact that the Mass liturgy for the fourth Sunday of Lent, *Laetare*, included the gospel of the multiplication of the loaves, and then, when we heard the deacon's reading, *this* report in *this* church, we were not prepared for the experience — impossible to anticipate: on the one hand, to be taken out of the present moment, but, on the other hand, to be taken back precisely to the place in which we now concretely found ourselves.

In the meantime, the last week of our pilgrimage had begun. Despite individual warnings, we boarded a boat that took us to the other shore of the lake, where we ate St. Peter's fish, and experienced on the return journey with what amazing rapidity the biblical "storm at sea" can arise on the completely calm surface of the lake. — Together with the Abbot we made the journey to Mount

Tabor, whose summit was veiled in thick cloud. Then an astonishingly peaceful border crossing directly at the fence that separates Israel from Lebanon; here there was never any shooting, Brother David assured us. In the last days we had a big sight-seeing journey organized by the hotel. It brought us far into and around Galilee. We saw fruit farms and irrigation installations, and realized that the continued threat by Syria that it would divert the Jordan River would mean war. In many a small town, a tank or a cannon was raised on a plinth as a memorial. In front of the synagogue of Safed, especially dear to the Jews because of its links with cabalism, there was a kind of triumphal arch on which, for the benefit of the clearly numerous tourists, in large letters beside the Hebrew text of the Sabbath ban was written, for practical purposes in English: *Don't smoke! Don't carry a camera!* In the meantime we knew about the ban on smoking; here we learned in addition that, on the Sabbath, taking photographs is not forbidden, but *carrying* a camera is.

But the special thing about this sightseeing tour was that we, again as the only non-Jews in the bus, heard an Israeli tour escort explaining to his co-believers also the Christian memorial sites. However, in Nazareth, in the still unfinished grandiose church of the Annunciation, a Franciscan was our guide. But the words engraved in a marble panel "Here the Word became flesh" did not, as in Bethlehem, take my breath away. Instead, quite apart from the highly problematic identifying of "Mary's House," a spontaneous protest arose in me against any attempt to localize this mysterious event. On the whole, Nazareth, like Chorazim and Capernaum, made a mournful impression on us. The rocky precipice down which they wanted to cast Jesus after he manifested himself in the temple can be seen today. "But he slipped through the crowd and walked away." He went into "his town," to Capernaum. For centuries Nazareth seems to have resisted the presence of Christians. Origen, who travelled around the whole of Palestine in the third century, never visited this town. Neither Constantine nor Helen built a church here. And today Nazareth is the headquarters of communism in Israel.

By chance it was the Sabbath when we left Tiberias. We were not surprised that in this hotel which was "under the scrutiny of the rabbis" no one would touch our luggage. But a taxi did bring us to Tel Aviv, where it was cold and there were storms. Early to bed. And the next morning, returning home via Zurich and Düsseldorf.

Shortly thereafter the summer semester would begin. The theme of my lecture was Plato's "Phaedo" dialog, which deals with the death of Socrates and the theme of immortality. For the pilgrimage we had undertaken in memory of the dead it was an epilogue unplanned, but telling.

II

Post-Conciliar Confusion

Councils have always been accompanied by great confusion — so said John Henry Newman in the context of a vigorous discussion about the First Vatican Council. More than thirty years before Vatican II, I had underlined these words in very thick pencil in my German edition of Newman's correspondence. Naturally, I did not realize what crucial significance it was to have for me personally. In what follows I shall be dealing with such confusions as were naturally to be expected — not in an attempt at definitiveness or completeness — but only insofar as they concerned me personally and annoyed, shocked, and provoked me to contradiction

My travel companion of old, the Leipzig Oratorian Werner Becker, said in a circular letter sent to his friends that Vatican II had fulfilled all his wishes. I replied to him that it was only possible to say this as long as one kept to what was expressly said in the Council's decrees, but not if one took into consideration what actually happened as a result of the Council — and often enough while appealing to its "spirit." This result was wretched impoverishment and even meaninglessness.

For example, we read in the liturgical constitution of the Council: "The Church regards Gregorian Chant as the music proper to the Roman liturgy." But where can we hear it and join in singing it? The requiem for our son Thomas, celebrated at the end of July 1964 — about a year and a half after the end of the Council — is, down to the present day, the last Mass in a parish church I can remember as being sung by the whole congregation in Gregorian Chant. — Anyone who does not have the good fortune to live in a town in which there is occasionally a parish priest who, without being a "traditionalist," celebrates a sung Mass every Sunday, must be living in a town where there is a bishop or must be able to visit a Benedictine monastery — if he is not to settle for listening to the (really excellent) recordings through which the monks of Münster-Schwarzach Abbey make accessible the choral masses for the great feast days in the church calendar. When hearing the music that everyone used to know, one becomes aware, not without sadness and shame, what immeasurable treasures Catholic Christendom has recklessly thrown away and has perhaps irrevocably lost.

Probably this loss has to do with the fact that Gregorian Chant and Latin belong together by nature. And the Liturgy Constitution can be quoted again, which requires things which are hardly compatible. On the one hand it says: "The use of the Latin language is to be retained"; on the other hand, "more room is to be given" to the vernacular language. With regard to this difficult theme, I am reminded of something which perhaps deserves to be retained. Before World War I, my father, while I sat beside him at the organ, had the local *schola* of a Westphalian village — remote from the world — Sunday for Sunday, sing a choral Mass; at that time the recurring songs of two or three choral Masses were once and for all imprinted on my memory so that, if they are sung today, I don't need to have either the text or the music in front of me. The cantor in those years was the blacksmith, who also sang while he worked, but naturally songs of a different kind. When he was in an especially celebratory mood at High Mass he would put a typically Münster rolled "r" into the *Amen*. But I will not easily be convinced that these singers and the congregation from the farming community did not understand what was meant by *Kyrie eleison*, and *Gloria*, *Credo* and *Sanctus*. — On the other hand, no one will

33

deny that to millions of Asian, African and also American Catholics the Latin language of worship will remain foreign.

But there is another seldom mentioned aspect that must also be looked at. I mean the irrevocably sacred character of liturgical language. The sacred implies difference and otherness over against ordinary normality which — and rightly so — governs our everyday life. The sacred explicitly involves separation from the trivial average nature of everyday life. This is comprehensible only to someone who is convinced that, in the midst of everyday existence, there is something that is radically not every day in nature, which is what we refer to in using a word like "mystery." It is the totally non-everyday of divine presence which naturally demands of man the answer of an "other" attitude — and an "other" way of speaking.

The defenders of a desacralized way of speaking – i.e., a way which, even in the church and in the Mass, approximates as closely as possible to, and is even identical with the average way of speaking — have occasionally, in debate with me, appealed to an official "Instruction" which allows and even recommends such freedom with language. Naturally I immediately chased down this document, which was not easy to find and, strangely, was written in French (25 January 1969), but I was not able find in it any trace of tolerance, let alone support for, trivial everyday speech. The theologically well-founded text does demand that translations into the vernacular must also be intelligible to ordinary people, but they, too, share the claim to be the "voice of the Church" that "speaks to its Lord"; and in the liturgy, it is said, the word is not purely a means of understanding but is "at the same time *mysterium*." It is therefore not only lacking in taste but it is contradictory to the essence of the liturgy to greet people at the beginning of Mass with "Good evening!" or, like the TV announcers, with "You are very welcome!" These are people who, on entering the church, bless themselves with Holy Water and genuflect before the Blessed Sacrament, and thereby enter into the "other," the "holy" sphere of our world. And so I find myself confirmed by the Church, in its own words, in doing what I have already sometimes done, and with success — i.e., in not accepting this kind of address.

With the word *mysterium*, which is always connected with the language of the liturgy, another aspect of sacred language has been named. It is difficult to define clearly, but it does have a concrete meaning. I am referring to the element of the veil by which the mystery is protected from the very direct threat of language. This is the point where something about the subject of foreign languages should be said, about which, these days, we probably have too little understanding. Through the medium of foreign languages something can be perceived or sensed which might otherwise be covered up by directly naming it. Here there is a certain analogy to the usual way of speaking about sexuality which, through its disrespectful physiologically focused character, meaning to give us "enlightenment," threatens to leave out a whole dimension of reality — namely the specifically human.

I don't know how often I have attended the Easter blessing of the baptismal water celebrated by the Bishop in St. Paul's Cathedral in Münster. I remember, above all, Clemens August von Galen, who, with his somewhat dull, tortured sounding voice as he let the Easter candle down into the water, sang on three different notes the words: *Descendat in hanc plenitudinem fontis virtus Spiritus Sancti.* Hundreds of people listened with deep, silent attention and observed the symbolic action; and I am convinced that here, despite the Latin language, what was mysteriously happening here was brought home to the simplest of Christians present in an incomparably moving way — much more than it could be by the completely clear new German text, which is sad, impoverished, and cold: "Let the power of the Holy Spirit descend into this water!" [Es steige hinab in dieses Wasser die Kraft des Heiligen

Geistes!] I am even afraid that when the incense boat is produced for what is now almost the only occasion in the year, the "young person of today" will not only not be involved, but will be more likely to ask whether that is not all "hocus pocus." The Bishop of Münster said to me, upset and in shock after the first time he performed the new rite, "If only I had at least been able to sing it!" The *Missale Romanum* speaks continually of the *plenitudo fontis*. To say instead "this water" is obviously a wretched abbreviation. But if it is too "poetic" to speak of this overflowing spring," why not in this particular case — and it might not be the only one — keep the Latin text and, of course, not speak it but sing it? In any case, here as elsewhere, translating into German giving the true meaning is the real problem, which often enough remains unsolved.

Naturally, in Germany there have been useful translations of the Mass for decades. Before World War II I myself collaborated on a German Sunday Missal which was taken up by three West German bishoprics and included for the first time in their official "Diocesan Prayer book"; that was something quite new. But now, after the Council, it was understandably necessary to provide an official translation of the missal to be used on the altar in all the German-speaking countries. For the first of these loosely planned beginnings of a far-reaching and difficult undertaking I was invited by my friend Joseph Pascher to collaborate. For many years he had been teaching in Munich. The Abbot of Maria Laach as well as the director of the Trier Liturgical Institute were members of the small team of translators which used to gather in Pascher's house. And, as was to be expected, there were extremely stimulating discussions backed by expertise. I soon withdrew, however, not only because of the impossibility of regular travel to Munich but, above all, because it very soon became clear to me that a group could not give such texts a unified character — at least in the first instance. This required a single competent individual. But then the team of collaborators was considerably expanded; naturally the Austrians and the German-speaking Swiss wanted to be represented. Besides, some especially important prayer texts should be made acceptable also to non-Catholic Christians — for example, the Our Father, the slightly altered new formulation of which can be seen as perhaps the only successful model of a valid translation.

What interested me most were the texts of the *Ordo Missae* — the translation of the prayers which occur in every celebration of the Mass; and here I suggested quite a few changes. Unfortunately only one of them was accepted by the relevant authority — and, of course, I don't know whether the same suggestion was put forward by other critics.

My objections concerned not so much inadequate linguistic formulations but primarily the destruction of meaning — which is almost always caused by misuse of language. When, for example, in the Offertory prayers it is said of the gifts of bread and wine: "We bring them before your face," two things are combined here: through vague, nondescript language the fundamentally human gesture is deprived of its right name. This name is, in Latin, *offerre* and *oblatio*. The words have a completely clear and precise meaning — which is spoken and at the same time realized: this, which belongs to me, is from now on no longer to be mine, but "yours"! I give up what was my property, was for my use, and hand it over to God for it to be at his disposal. Something given in this way cannot be taken back — whether it is the coin put into the collection box or the candle lit in front of the statue of the Madonna, or the flowers given to decorate the altar, and, above all, the gifts of bread and wine brought in celebration by the congregation.

I think I know fairly exactly the reasons for avoiding the word translating *oblation* [Darbringung]: first, there is the desire to avoid giving even the slightest support to the (false) notion that the Catholic Church understands the Mass as a "repetition" of the one sacrifice which took place once and for all on Golgotha. But second, what is really missing is the clear distinction between the *oblatio* and *sacrificium* in the strict sense of cultic sacrifice. And for me personally, I must confess, this fundamental distinction became clear only in India when I took part in the opening of the Durga Festival in the square of the Kali Temple in Calcutta. On the one hand there was the stream of festively clothed people striving to reach the entrance to the temple in order to hand over to the priest the gifts they carried in their raised hands in a liturgical gesture: hibiscus blooms, rice, and mangos, all laid out on fresh leaves. This was an act of oblation to which people are often and naturally driven. Then something of a fundamentally different kind happened in another part of the temple area, exactly in front of the eyes of the Goddess (who did remain hidden): the ritual slaying of a young goat, a *sacrificium* in the exact sense of the word.

Another example, which especially provoked my likewise unsuccessful protest was and is the translation of the text which immediately follows the Consecration and begins with the words *Unde et memores*. Josef Andreas Jungmann has called it "the central sacrificial prayer of the entire Mass liturgy." But having any awareness of precisely this particular quality is made virtually impossible for the ordinary listener and reader because of the now officially accepted German version. It can, in fact, also for another reason, serve as a model case of a translation which distorts meaning. There are two objections which I have raised against it, neither of which, as I have said, was accepted. — First, we find realized here the especially dubious notion on which the whole translation is fundamentally based: namely, that the ordinary Christian can be expected to understand two successive main clauses but not some kind of more challenging sentence structure. This supposition, which at first seems to be one of a purely linguistic and psychological kind, has in reality — as this example shows — far-reaching consequences. In the present translation the prayer begins with the words: "Therefore we celebrate the memory ..." The truth is that the word *unde* refers to the bringing of the sacrificial gift, which is Christ himself; precisely this is the "act" which the Lord enjoined upon his apostles. But the translation almost enforces what we know as the widespread error that the Mass is essentially a commemorative celebration and not an act that makes Jesus Christ's sacrifice on the cross present amongst us.

The second objection is that the original text — and also the new addition — has no mention at all of "celebrating" the memory, but quite simply and soberly speaks of being mindful. The completely clear meaning of the prayer, which is supposedly beyond the comprehension of normal people, is as follows: "Therefore Lord, being mindful of Your Son we bring you the holy bread of eternal life and the chalice of perpetual salvation." This latter formulation, as everyone can see, is not to be found in the current translation. The festive aspect of the language recedes precisely at the only point where the original text sees it as meaningful. The sacrifice of Jesus Christ, which is what is truly to be celebrated, is spoken about with all the hymnic exuberance belonging to sacred language, and the repetitions are also a part of this ("the pure sacrifice, the holy sacrifice, the spotless sacrifice.") But all of this is left out or abbreviated, probably because the rationalists mistook the exuberant for the superfluous and saw in it only empty words.

How the *unde* (therefore) is to be understood and what alone it refers to has been explained in the moving words of Thomas Aquinas which have been passed over all too easily — at first by myself as well. When the priest, in using this word, appeals to the role assigned him by the Lord, he is excusing himself for undertaking something so prodigious as making present in the mysterious celebration of the Mass the sacrificial death of Christ. In the *Summa theologica* Thomas uses the term *excusat praesumptionem* [excuses himself for the presumption].

In the official translation of one of the Eucharistic prayers it is said of the dead that they "have gone to sleep in the hope that they will rise again." I protested against this formulation with particular vigor, but again in vain. "Who does not see," I said quite aggressively, "that here the objective aspect of the *spes resurrectionis* [hope of resurrection] is lost from sight and comes close to a purely subjective, possibly vain hope." The answer I received — with some justification — was that it did not sound good to speak of "hope of resurrection." I was pleased to find that both leaders of the translation commission agreed with my counter suggestion: " ... went to sleep in the hope of a blessed resurrection." They also immediately accepted my reasons for including the word "blessed" [selig]: namely, that in the Bible there is also mention of "resurrection for judgment." But this agreement, which seemed to be without qualification, was not enough to warrant inclusion in the final version of the text published later.

Of my numerous contributions, the only one which could convince the authorities was my objection to the avoidance of the word *mysterium*. The Latin version of the *Ordo Missae*, also at first deemed to be provisional, suggested three different formulations for the summons to confession of guilt with which the Mass begins. In an early German translation there were four formulations, in which, however, the crucial words corresponding to the Latin were simply left out. In this, I am convinced, a frailty came to light that was characteristic of theological thinking not only of "those days." In a kind of "phobia," mention of the "holy mysteries" was left out, for the festive celebration of which we were to purify ourselves by our confession of guilt: *ut apti simus ad sacra mysteria celebranda*. Still, in today's call to the confession of guilt as it is found in the German altar missal there is also mention of the "right way" to celebrate the "holy mysteries" [Geheimnisse].

There is a particularly crass case of arbitrary translation which can also be explained only by the almost pathological fear of calling the holy by its right name. I first became aware of this when the discussion about translating the *Ordo Missae* into German had long since been concluded and the German altar missal printed — and the futility of any subsequent protest was evident. But I cannot omit raising this protest. It concerns the German translation of the word *consecratio*, by which already in pre-Christian Rome, according to the *Oxford Classical Dictionary*, the act is one through which something is changed into a *res sacra*, something holy. The term used formerly [Wandlung] applies very exactly to the event that constitutes the climax of the sacred action in the Mass. But how is *consecratio* in the *Institutio Generalis* of the new altar missal translated into German? Unbelievably by the term "narrative of institution" [Einsetzungsbericht] which, as no one will deny, is nothing but the neutral designation for an historical process. I see this "translation," which destroys the original meaning, simply as a scandal. And here we see the unbroken virulence of the poison of "desacralization." This is found everywhere, from the statements in conferences on Church architecture — where it is said, and almost taken for granted, that of course the church is not a sacred space — to doubts about the consecrating power conferred on the priest in the Sacrament of Holy Orders.

This is the place to describe something which happened in our ecumenical work group, and which ultimately persuaded me no longer to take part in the conferences. In spring 1951 the Evangelical group, not without a certain secretiveness, sought to dedicate the first half hour of the opening session to a special "act." Only a few initiates knew what was to happen: namely, that Peter Brunner would stand up and, this time not as a member of the circle but with a solemnity that was not usual with him, as Dean of the Heidelberg Theology Faculty confer an honorary doctorate on Heinz Dietrich Wendland, who had joined the group for the first time. Wendland was at that time still Professor of New Testament theology in Münster. He had only recently returned from Russia, where he had been a prisoner of war, and was unknown to most of us. Both the Latin charter and the eulogy spoken gave him special praise for the spiritual help given to his fellow prisoners. Honored in this way — clearly to his complete surprise — he expressed his thanks. He was deeply moved and scarcely able to control his voice. But what he said was perfectly formulated.

At the time I did not realize, and Wendland himself probably never found out, how important — not just for me but for the whole work group — one single sentence was to be, which, more than fifteen years later, he formulated in answer to a question I had very seriously raised. Wendland had in the meantime changed disciplines and taken over the "Institute for Christian Social Sciences" which had been created in the Faculty of Evangelical Theology shortly after his return, and presumably for this reason he was elected to the "Rhine-Westphalian Academy of Sciences," which at that time was still called the "Arbeitsgemeinschaft für Forschung." Wendland's inaugural lecture in this circle in January 1967 was entitled "The ecumenical movement and the Second Vatican Council." On the return journey from Düsseldorf to Münster we happened to be sharing the same compartment and for the whole two hours we were alone. Naturally, we spoke about his lecture. I said I found it interesting that, unusually, it was driven by a theological and religious impulse. He seemed pleased enough to hear this. This was the beginning of the first and only lengthy and very personal conversation which we had with one another and in which he made the important utterance. Amongst other things, I asked him about his time as a prisoner of war. He immediately spoke about it at length. He came to speak of the difficulty of celebrating the Eucharist. One of his religious brethren had, for example, since there was naturally no wine available, used water or tea instead. Then he had said to himself, if it is going to be done at all then under one species: bread! Now that the conversation was touching on ultimate questions I could not help asking, with all due caution: "What, in your opinion, happens with the bread in such a Eucharistic celebration?" Suddenly, with excited gestures, Wendland said emphatically: "No one in the Evangelical Church is able to tell me what powers I receive at ordination." It was clear that he was speaking of the powers of consecration. Soon the journey, and with it the conversation, was at an end.

Three years later, spring 1970. The ecumenical work group, meeting in Tutzing, was discussing the theme "Intercommunion." After the contributions of the exegetes there was a wide-ranging discussion of the question whether the "so-called" Last Supper was fundamentally different from other meals with Jesus — and from which no one was excluded from participating. And so why limit admission to the celebration of Mass (Abendmahl) and the Eucharist? Finally, I put up my hand to speak. Intending to use the freedom of the gown which, for better or for worse, had been granted to me as the only layman in the Catholic group for many years, I asked a very simple question. I described how, during my American semester as guest professor, I had attended several services: first the Catholic one, which was externally the most wretched one, and then one or two musically and ritually absolutely superb "services" of other denominations. But it had never entered my mind to take part in the communion. "Why not? Because I wanted to receive the true body of the Lord!" But this was not to be had here and for no other reason than that the "celebrant" did not have the power to consecrate. In the midday break which immediately followed my intervention, some of my Catholic colleagues attacked me with more or less kindly irony — although, as I am still convinced today, I had said nothing different from what was in the Ecumenical Decree of Vatican II, which clearly says: "in the separated Church communities" there is no sacrament of Holy Orders, for which reason the original and complete reality (*substantia*) of the Eucharistic mystery has not been retained. One man put a friendly arm around my shoulder and said: "You are the last Catholic!" From another professor of Catholic Theology came the absurd question whether I really believed that as a priest one could "consecrate the contents of a whole baker's shop."

After the midday meal and a siesta, all of that seemed at first to be forgotten. But surprisingly, an Evangelical theologian wanted my question discussed from the opposite direction — and concretely and provocatively! He suggested that his co-believers present should say why they would not go to communion at a Catholic Mass. The amazing thing was that none of those who spoke would go, although some, amongst them Peter Brunner, clearly expressed their conviction that in the Eucharistic celebration of the Catholic Church the true body of the Lord is offered and received. The discussion sparked by this brought up a whole bundle of accusations against the Catholic Church which up to now could not have been aired in our group. Unexpectedly, we found ourselves embroiled in an unusually sharp debate. Even my friend Hermann Volk, who had been Bishop of Mainz for eight years, banged his hand on the table and, temperamentally, put a few things straight. The usually very quiet Bishop Wilhelm Stählin, who together with Cardinal Lorenz Jäger was the co-founder of the workgroup and, from the beginning, President of the Evangelical group, was silent now as well. Only at the end of the conference was he to give, as it turned out, his definitive opinion.

At the evening meal where we sat in rotation at tables of six, Wendland and I were sitting opposite one another. He had said nothing during the day's discussions. I asked him across the table, so that all must have heard, whether he remembered the conversation we had had years ago on our journey from Düsseldorf to Münster. He replied with a very definite yes. "Would you today stand by what you said then: 'No one in the Evangelical Church ...'?" He would not let me finish and repeated the statement word for word. And yes, he stood by it very definitely.

The next day, at the end of the conference, Bishop Stählin spoke. In a clear, precise speech he tried to formulate a conclusion to be drawn from this gathering — which was to be his last. It was his intention, as an eighty-five-year-old, to resign his office and to take no part in further conferences. He introduced his successor, the military Bishop Hermann Kunst, who had arrived the day before in an Army helicopter. But he had saved up the most important thing for his final words: namely, the suggestion, which he wanted to be understood as his urgent farewell request, that next year's conference be devoted exclusively to the theme *Sacerdotium* [priesthood]. He was convinced that this was an inevitable consequence of the discussion which had just concluded. Of course, he said, at this point it was hardly possible to propose an alternative theme. Some did make the suggestion to treat Stählin's theme more broadly and speak generally of "office" in the Church. But Stählin found that enough had been said about this already and stayed with his suggestion. And so it was decided that the theme for the next conference was to be "priesthood."

However, in the spring of 1971 the Evangelical exegetes and systematic theologians, as was to be expected, presented their thesis about the non-existence of any official priesthood of their own — as something obvious and to be taken for granted — whereas, on the Catholic side, the teaching of the Second Vatican Council that the distinction between consecrated priesthood and general priesthood is not gradual but essential was not mentioned at all, let alone justified or defended. Wendland was not present, so that I did not feel I was committing any indiscretion — since several members of the circle had heard him confirm only a year ago what he had said previously — in taking the floor and telling our strange story in some detail. It was listened to in silence. There was no comment. No reaction. Cardinal Jaeger, on principle, never contributed to the discussion of themes. Bishop Kunst took me aside at the break and said it was incomprehensible to him how Wendland could have said such a thing, since at ordination appointment by the congregation was quite clearly expressed. But appointment and consecration are two different things.

That is when I made the decision no longer to take part in the conferences of the circle. On returning home I wrote to Cardinal Jaeger, saying how surprised and disappointed I was at the incomprehensible silence of our theologians. He answered immediately, saying he was deeply dissatisfied with the events at the conference and was ashamed at the thought that all of this was also due to be published. In a postscript he asked whether I would be prepared to write something myself on the theme of "priesthood." My spontaneous answer was that that was, after all, not my trade. I later changed my mind and did in fact publish a "necessary attempt at clarification" (What distinguishes the priest?). And I did not omit to say what was behind my decision to write the piece. My thesis, based on Thomas Aquinas and the Second Vatican Council, was briefly this: a person does not become a priest by "appointment of the congregation"; priests are consecrated (*sacerdotes consecrantur*) in order to carry out the sacrament of the Body of Christ.

A Berlin prelate who accompanied Cardinal Alfred Bengsch to Rome for the Synod of Bishops let me know that his Cardinal had presented the *opusculum* to the Pope with the comment that latterly in Germany only a layman had anything adequate to say on the theme of "priesthood."

But now I have still to report on America, the land of my worst experiences of "post-conciliar confusion." When in our ecumenical workgroup in our free social evenings I had to report on my journeys, especially to America, the question naturally arose as to whether there were any inter-confessional theological conversations. With some exaggeration, I answered: "No! Because over there they have no theology — at least, no Catholic theology!" And, indeed, this was in 1950 my first big surprise: at the hundreds of Catholic universities in the country there was no Faculty of Theology — apart, of course, from the one in Washington supported by the entire episcopate. Future priests did not at all study at a university but in mostly remote seminaries of the dioceses and of the religious orders — at which, of course, excellent professors taught. But the very word "ecumenical" (for example) was largely eschewed in these institutions. A German theologian, a priest who immediately after World War II was sent by the German bishops to the United States seeking financial support for church aid programs, told me that in his many lectures at Catholic universities and seminaries two themes were expressly designated as simply "impossible": "ecumenism" and "liturgy." Under those circumstances how could there be any controversial theological conversations? But there was, on the other hand – in an atmosphere of mutual respect — unproblematic human collaboration between the Christian denominations in social and charitable work. Often there was praise for the discreet and natural way it was arranged: for example, that fish dishes be served to Catholic delegates if one of the organizing committees happened to be meeting for a meal on a Friday. Here I am touching on a nerve which concerns me at this point. I am convinced that it has to do with the especially ominous confusions of the post-conciliar period – something the Europeans find hard to understand. Perhaps it is to be ascribed to the Irish influence — which is often enough to be found in that country — that Friday was a "day of abstinence" and the whole of the Lenten period of fasting had become a kind of public institution, binding not only on Catholics but on everyone. Even in the most exclusive restaurants in Chicago, during the Church's fasting period guests would, along with the normal menu, be presented with the "fasting menu." And since the dinner in honor of Theodor Heuss happened to fall on a Friday the guests in New York's Waldorf Astoria were offered a — naturally exquisite — meal of fish. I don't remember ever seeing a New York drugstore that did not, on Thursday every week, clearly advertise a "Friday Menu," i.e., a meal without meat. This is certainly astonishing in the land of steaks which were usually promoted with details about their considerable size. And now imagine, just two weeks after the ceremonial closure of the Council an easing of the regulation was announced: it was no longer binding; instead one was free either to make a "Friday sacrifice" in the form of a work of charity or piety of some sort in place of the law of abstinence. Also elsewhere in the world, for example in Germany, through a "de-concretizing" of this kind — as a bishop recently aptly described it — Friday as a day commemorating Jesus Christ's death on the cross has in fact been abolished. But in America this annulment of the Friday tradition, incomprehensible to the average Christian, held far greater meaning: if this was no longer binding, then nothing was! In this way, in fact, a mighty landslide was caused which radically changed and disfigured the face of Catholic life in this country — which was already experiencing many problems. And in 1967, when I was on my way to Canada and was visiting an American university for the first time in five years after my departure from Stanford, I was somewhat confused and thrown when confronted with this puzzling change.

At Brown University, Louis Bouyer was lecturing for a while. I had met him briefly in Paris. In the guest house of the university he tried to answer my amazed question about what, in his opinion, had really happened in this country. He said that the Second Vatican Council had, with its decrees, burst on the ill-prepared American Catholics like a storm. Precisely in the spheres of ecumenism and liturgy there were the most unbelievable reactions. For example, because "ecumenism" was not understood, a well-known Protestant theologian was invited by a large Catholic university to teach in a summer course. To the wild applause of an auditorium of nuns he announced "the death of God." And with regard to the liturgy: "Masses" were celebrated without the canon and consecration. There were priests who referred to the Incarnation as a "myth" — and so on. To a large extent the bishops were not sufficiently educated in theology and were afraid, above all, of being considered backward. That was the unbelievable information which Louis Bouyer gave me.

The visit to the great St. John's Benedictine Abbey in

Minnesota in spring 1968 was a particularly depressing experience. My youngest son and I were thinking of spending a peaceful Holy Week and Easter there. I had already been a guest there for a few days in 1950 and I have a clear memory of the way the old Abbot, now many years dead, invited me, with his old-fashioned courteous words, to honor him by taking my meals at his table in the refectory in silence, *sub silentio*. In the meantime, a new Abbey Church based on plans by Marcel Breuer had been erected at the cost of some millions of dollars. It was, indeed, the most impressive sacred building on the whole continent. But in the meantime the desacralization germ had shown its virulence here, at St. John's university, which considered itself a "Center for Liturgical Studies." This became clear to us at our first visit to the church. When I knelt down in the chapel of the Blessed Sacrament the monk who was accompanying me said almost apologetically that, unfortunately, the bishop had demanded that there be a tabernacle in the church. — Even the greeting by G. D., the initiator of the liturgical revival in America, soon proved to be a great disappointment. I had felt we were almost friends since, in 1950, we strolled through the windy streets of Chicago in almost breathless conversation, continually finding ourselves in agreement about our convictions. Naturally, we found ourselves immediately caught up in theological discussion, and with consternation I heard that the sacramental teaching of the Church should be revised; on the one hand, reading the Bible was also sacramental; and on the other hand, there were only two sacraments: baptism and the Eucharist. Besides, the new church building was to be used for generally "shared human" activities. During the Divine Office, at which, when no one was on supply elsewhere, two hundred monks were participating, Latin, as well as Gregorian Chant — and even the *tonus rectus* — had been abolished. Each person spoke in his own individual way, holding a couple of copied pages of text. The doxology, i.e. the *Gloria Patri*, at the end of each psalm and at which you would stand and bow, had likewise been omitted as an "unbiblical extra." At the Holy Thursday service the washing of the feet was gone: the symbolism was thought to be "too cheap." In the refectory there was an "Easter Meal" at which bread and then wine blessed by the Abbot were ritually consumed during certain readings. G. D. looked at me in surprised incomprehension when I questioned whether this was not simply "pseudo-liturgy," since precisely this "Easter Meal" was in truth celebrated in High Mass on Holy Thursday. On Good Friday the story of the Passion was neither sung nor even spoken in separate roles but read unceremoniously by one individual monk — and indeed in a trivial English translation, in which, for example, Judas does not say "Greetings, Master" (*Ave, Rabbi*) but *Good evening*. The Easter Night *Exultet*, by its very nature one single entire song of praise, was reduced to a third and was spoken in a most ordinary everyday tone. My son, not having accommodation like mine in the comfortably appointed new guest wing but in a monk's cell in the monastery, brought his book and took refuge in my room in order to have peace on what was known in Westphalia as "quiet Friday" and to escape the loud noise of cheap radio music booming out of a neighboring monk's cell. For reading at table the "Dutch Catechism" was used — in a rushed English translation which had not undergone the due correction required by the Vatican. On the morning we left, winter had returned with a heavy snowfall. Shivering and sad we took our leave. We had never experienced such drab Easter ceremonies.

But the bitterest disappointment was still some years ahead of me. A visit to the priory of my friend L. R. was long overdue. I arrived there on a hot summer's day just half an hour before the regular celebration of Mass in the late afternoon. The priory was a confused group of faceless buildings which looked as if they had been thrown together without a plan. The first person to greet me was Brother David whom I knew from Israel and liked. He was just returning home and was climbing down from a tractor.

Contributing to his fantastic appearance was a gaudy pair of flimsy
Bermuda shorts. Soon my friend appeared. He had returned here
and was now called "Abt-Abt." He was dressed in undistinguished
civilian clothes and wore a red pullover under a red summer jacket.
Mass was soon to begin. Because of the large crowds it was not to
be celebrated in the chapel but in a barn provisionally arranged for
the purpose. For the moment there was little time for a conversation. I was astonished to see the monks enter the barn, some of
whom I had just seen wearing the most unlikely and varied clothing but all of them now in a broad white garment which was clearly
modelled on the Benedictine cuculle; I heard later that they were
now planning the same garment in blue. One of the monks was
carrying a guitar, to the accompaniment of which everyone sang a
song created by a musically highly-gifted member of the community. This song was attracting many visitors. Records of it were
also available for sale. The barn was packed, above all, it seemed,
by tourists who had summer residences nearby. You could see that
a good number of them were not used to attending a Catholic
Mass. With some surprise I noticed that the priest did not start
the Mass with the usual sign of the cross and the accompanying
words. As yet I did not know that this was on principle. During
the whole celebration of the Mass I did not see a sign of the cross
— not even during the consecration. It was the same when grace
was said at the meal in the refectory which I was invited to attend.
It was also clearly no longer the custom to kneel, even after the
consecration. Instead of a sermon interpreting the word of God
and resulting from contemplation and study, the congregation was
called upon to express thoughts which had come to them more or
less by chance during the reading of the gospel. It was simply a
scandal the way the arbitrarily adjusted Eucharist Prayer spoke of
"Jesus, our Brother," who "during a meal with His friends took
bread" – and so on. For the communion the celebrant walked a few
steps in front of the altar, with a big round plate full of pieces of

bread and, with a friendly smile, invited "anyone who wants to join us" to partake. And that is what happened. There was no mention of this being the "Body of Christ." Then two of the monks — few of whom were priests — came and stood to either side of the celebrant and offered a communion chalice to anyone who wanted it. Naturally the chalices were soon empty; but they were immediately filled again from containers which were kept at the ready on a table near the wall of the barn. After the service, as the barn was gradually emptying I remained conversing with a group of monks. They greeted me, and some of them knew one or other of my books. While one of them jokingly said that he had not imagined the author to be so tall and slim, I noticed, somewhat concerned, that he was holding one of the chalices, still one third full, dangling loosely in his hand. I was thinking: full of what?

Once outside, where some of the monks had taken off their white garments and donned their workday civilian clothes, full of anger I made a beeline to my friend to say to him that I was not at all sure I had been at a real Mass. "Are people in this monastery not aware that in the Catholic Mass the priest gives a person the consecrated host and says the words: 'The Body of Christ' — which is not just announcing something, but is at the same time a warning?" Perhaps I came on too strong, and the long debate which followed was not without bitterness. It concerned the reality of the consecration, the difference between "friends" and "apostles," the meaning of the sign of the cross and physical signs as such; and finally I reminded my friend of the sung Mass celebrated every evening years ago in Tabgha. But my friend, surprised and disconcerted by my outburst which even surprised me, accepted none of my criticism. Later I sent him one of my articles [Buchstabier-Übungen] entitled "Jesus, our Brother?" In his answer he said it was, of course, clear to him that this was aimed at the Mass in his monastery; but my arguments had not convinced him. — Eight years later, for his eightieth birthday my friend received from his monks the marvelous present of a trip to Jerusalem and then to his native Westphalian Abbey. From there I received a phone call on Whit Tuesday 1982 that Abbot L. was in the university clinic in Münster for a medical examination and would like me to visit him there. When I inquired, I was told by the Director of the clinic that they were waiting for the driver, a monk, who would bring the Abbot to me. "But I'll come myself and we can walk to my house. It is only a few minutes away." "No, our patient would not manage that." Surprised and worried, I saw my friend shortly afterwards, dressed now in the normal Benedictine habit, walking with difficulty up the steps to my garden terrace. Over a glass of wine three of us had a brief conversation. There was no mention of our American disputes. The Abbot had already clambered back into the car and I was trying to explain to the monk now sitting at the wheel why it had been years since I visited their monastery, in which over a period of years I had been a guest in my student days, sometimes staying for weeks. The reason, I said, was the fear that here, as well, there would have been too many changes. The monk vigorously denied it. The Abbot had heard us and said, as the car was about to drive away: "Here things are different from over there!" In farewell, I jokingly answered with a threatening gesture; joking, but both of us knew the seriousness behind it. The continuation of our debate, vaguely referred to in this gesture, never occurred. A few weeks later I read in the newspaper that the Abbot had died of bone cancer in a Boston hospital.

III

Detours to the Aquinas Medal

It was literally for the conferring of this medal named after my teacher, Thomas Aquinas, that I set out, in the middle of March 1968, for New Orleans in the American state of Louisiana. The letter which communicated to me the awarding of the prize was accompanied by the request that, if possible, I should come to receive it personally. They would not be able to pay for my flight across the Atlantic, but there would not be the slightest problem in organizing a lecture tour throughout the country. I immediately agreed to this and soon sketched out the itinerary I envisaged. Besides, my son Michael, who was a sociology student and who had just turned twenty-six, wanted to come with me. Both of us kept a travel diary. A comparison soon shows that things and people were seen very differently by father and son.

Our planned start in the Northwest of America, in Washington State, had nothing to do with any kind of extravagance on my part. Our intention was, rather, to visit the city of Seattle, in which Thomas, our son and brother, had died four years previously. The non-stop flight from Copenhagen to Seattle via Greenland and Canada was particularly fascinating because, as we looked south out the window, we could see the sun always at its highest point in the sky. It was continuously midday. We took off shortly after twelve and, according to local time, it was not yet one o'clock when we landed almost eight thousand kilometers away in Seattle. The next day, during a visit to the Boeing Airplane Works, an engineer

54

said to us that they were now in the process of building an airplane with which we would leave Copenhagen at twelve o'clock and arrive in Seattle three hours earlier at nine o'clock.

Of course, something else was of far greater interest to me. After a short, deep sleep — my son could not emerge from his — I slipped away quietly to the King County Hospital into which Thomas had been delivered at the end of July 1964 and which he had never left alive. It was fairly close to our hotel and in the direct neighborhood of the cathedral, which — it now seemed strange to me — I had visited twice, in 1950 and 1962. It was situated high above the city and overlooked the port and the sea. In the hospital I made inquiries and found my way to the neurosurgical department, but the doctor who had performed the operation and whom I had phoned about the "the post-mortem examination" was no longer known there. Deep in thought, I walked around the enormous building. At the back of it at the emergency entrance, an ambulance was arriving; "just as in that night," I thought. But then Goethe's words came to mind: "In every great separation there is a grain of madness; one must be careful not to let it hatch out and then dwell on it." And so I went for a few minutes into the cathedral and back to the hotel. I then went for a stroll with my son in the city, where the flowers and trees in gardens and parks were, because of the sea current — as we were told — already in bloom before the spring. Although there were hardly any significant sights in this beautiful city we had not seen, I somehow had the feeling, when we were standing at the airport on a late afternoon some days later and were out in the open waiting for our next flight to be called, that I had missed something, although I could not say what it was. Unexpectedly, the riddle was solved: the cloud cover suddenly opened up and one of the most beautiful snow-peaks in the world came out into the sunlight, with the whole city at its feet: it was the broad, more than four thousand meters high peak of Mount Rainier, which had been fateful for Thomas. My son

55

Michael beamed also and we were both happy to be able to contemplate it for quite some time on the flight to San Francisco.

In San Francisco a rather strange interlude awaited us. Months ago a colleague had brought me three or four books from San Francisco as a present from an author I did not know. In each of the books he had written by hand a hymnic dedication to me as the author of *Leisure, the Basis of Culture*. As I paged through the books they seemed to me to set out and to defend a rather unreal utopian social view ("Everyone a capitalist!"). Naturally I expressed my gratitude for them to the author, whose name I found in the quite exclusive *Who's Who in the World*. At the same time I innocently mentioned my intention soon to visit San Francisco myself. This brought about the urgent request that I ring him without delay on my arrival. I did so, the morning after our arrival, from the cheap little hotel we had found near the bus station. Since I had only glanced through the books I was relieved to hear that the author would not be in the city for a few days, so I sent him my greetings and wanted to go. But I did not get out of it so easily. Immediately a collaborator of his introduced herself. She was even a co-author of a book and was clearly given the task of looking after me. The first thing was the very precisely formulated request that we dress to be guests of her boss in the Bohemian Club where she would collect us for dinner in the evening. She also asked me to make a note of the exact address of the Club. This turned out to be necessary, since there was nothing to identify the house except the bronze letters B.C. set into the footpath in front of the entrance. Discreetly uniformed employees, who observed, with an air of disapproval, that we carried in our own luggage, brought us into each of our excellently appointed quarters. My son was just in time for an almost all-day Sightseeing Tour through San Francisco and its environs, while I drove out alone — and I wanted to be alone — to Berkeley and the campus of the state university of California. Because of the holiday time it was almost empty of people; still, I

56

can remember some quite exotic figures: for example, a young, highly pregnant student in a long, bright evening dress with a plunging neckline. I set out in search of the Hearst Mining Building in which Thomas had worked. It was completely quiet; yet all the doors were open; here and there, behind a typewriter, a secretary immersed in her book and not to be disturbed. In my jacket pocket I had a color photo which Thomas had proudly sent us in the first weeks after his arrival. It shows him at work at the electron microscope. Strolling through the cellar area, I was suddenly standing in front of this gigantic research instrument which had always remained a mystery to me. Still no one was to be seen far and wide. But in the office of the professor to whom I had written there was a letter waiting for me, an invitation to a midday meal the following day.

Still ahead of us was the meeting that evening with my social utopian's collaborator. At the arranged time we were waiting in the hall of the B.C.; but then the aristocratic porter explained to us that the lady would well know that she could not enter the house — not even the entrance lobby. "This is a men's club!" And indeed we met the lady standing quite calmly outside the door beside a waiting taxi which drove us immediately to another "private" Club-Restaurant for an exquisite evening meal. The lady discreetly passed over the scandalous news that I was not able to express a reasoned opinion about the *opus* of her boss. Instead she expatiated, full of temperament, on her own views, above all about America. "If you were to find the Vietnam War good I would ignore you!" All the big words New Deal (Roosevelt), New Frontier (Kennedy), Great Society (Johnson) were only different names for one and the same thing: namely, the American "work slave state." "I am ashamed to be American." — For heaven's sake, what was I to say?!

The meal on the following day was an absolutely cheerful and unproblematic event when we met with Thomas's still astoundingly young teacher in the shaded garden of the Faculty Club.

There is much that I can say about him. Above all, there were the social evenings at which Thomas brought the whole team into high spirits and was himself the star entertainer — something which I heard in silent surprise, thinking my own thoughts. Student unrest, just now in the headlines again when the previous night on the Berkeley campus the mast of high tension wires was blown up, seemed of little interest to our relaxed host. Students in the sciences had far too much work to do for them to become involved. Laughing and groaning we finally squeezed ourselves into the cramped space of the professor's two-seater, whereupon he good-naturedly insisted on driving us to the nearest bus stop.

In the evening, my series of lectures in San Francisco began. My son Michael wandered through the much spoken-of little park in which the hippies, then called "flower children," used to gather. To judge by the way he described what he had seen and heard, his curiosity was rather quickly satisfied.

The next stop was Stanford where a more than expected enthusiastic reunion with former acquaintances awaited me. Amongst them was the famous agronomist Karl Brandt who, as I found out only later, was working as a government advisor on every continent. He is also the one who, a day or so later, with obvious pleasure brought us to the San Francisco airport in his luxurious car; and in fact we would only with difficulty have reached our check-in counter on time if he had not authoritatively ushered us through the channels reserved for VIPs. The spacious halls were completely blocked by supporters of the presidential candidate Robert Kennedy. Crowds of girls, above all, were pouring by, jumping up and down and repeating in chorus: "We want to see Bobby!" Like anyone else, they were not to know that the man they were celebrating would be murdered two months later.

The Grand Canyon was far off our course to Tucson in Arizona, but this incomparable, inverted mountain range (so to speak) dug into the depths of the earth, was definitely not to be denied to my travel companion Michael. We arrived just at sunset and contemplated in amazement the gradual transformation of the darkening colors from red to the still gleaming blue-grey and finally to the black of night. As we continued our onward journey and landed next in Phoenix we were suddenly torn from that land of the past into the historical present, when, on the face of an international clock, we were startled to see, along with Paris, London, Rome and New York, the name Vietnam, so that we were forced to wonder for what (and to whom) on this early spring morning of 1968 the hour was striking on the Mekong Delta.

One of my students from Notre Dame in 1950 had invited me to Tucson — and he thought he would immediately recognize me at the airport. But we had already gone past him when a young man caught up with us and brought us back to a man sitting in a wheel-chair, who was scarcely able to reach out his hand to greet us; but his eyes sparkled with keen intelligence, and his friendly greeting showed no signs of disability. The young man, clearly a student, brought the lamed man to a waiting car, carried him like a child in his arms and lifted him in; then he stowed the wheel-chair in the back of the car and got into the driver's seat. At first we were unable to say much, but then it became clear that we had met a most unusual man.

There was another surprise in store for us. We were set down in front of a house, at the door of which Philip Burnam greeted me. I had not at all expected to see him here. He said he would be glad to put at our disposal for a few days the newly-built guest wing of his beautiful bungalow. We would even be the first to live in it. Exactly twelve years ago he had organized an autographing party for me in his bookshop in San Francisco, near Union Square. I was completely unfamiliar with this procedure: offering a glass of wine to every purchaser of a book I was to sign. And now, after such a long time, the unexpected reunion was celebrated by a festive meal at which, above all, we learned extraordinary things about the initiator of this journey to Tucson who was still something of a mystery to us. Shortly before the end of his studies he was struck down with poliomyelitis and would have been shut out of all intellectual activity forever if his father had not insisted on pulling out the plug of the iron lung and then making him endure an inevitable moment of the most intense fear of death. In this way he had got back his life. His life did remain unspeakably difficult. Not only did he, from now on, need a constant helper to serve him with every mouthful, but — something that seemed unbelievable to us — he also had to sleep in a kind of rocking bed to avoid suffocation. Before going to sleep, we were told, he would listen to records of modern literature — T. S. Eliot's *Four Quartets*, for example. At the university he organized a series of Newman Lectures; my lecture was also part of the series. He had translated into English Maritain's book *Paysan de la Garonne*. At the end of this panegyric we heard something simply admirable: despite being plagued by this hardly bearable disability he travelled all over the world, bringing that bed everywhere, which, however, necessitated excluding countries in which the electricity supply was not reliable. — It was almost unreal to see one evening, in a gathering of dinner guests at a house of which he was the sole occupant, how his helper, in demonstrative silence, literally fed him, and how he himself then made a brilliantly formulated speech spiced with many witty references to current events.

But these days in Arizona were also full of other surprises. Near Tucson, for example, there is a 2000-meter-high mountain peak, on which, we were told, in several observatories maintained there by the universities of Harvard, Princeton, Yale and Chicago more work in astronomy was done than anywhere else in the world. And, of course, as is always the case in such American institutions, there is also something of interest for the layman to see. For instance, by means of a "helioscope" it is possible for anyone to project onto a white screen the real sun as it is in a normally cloudless sky and, without being blinded by the brightness, to look at the spots on the sun and its glimmering borders. And, by the way, this astronomy mountain lies in the middle of a Papago reservation. These Indians had not only to be paid a considerable rent, but they had also secured a contractual agreement to have the mountain peak to themselves for one week in the year to celebrate there their ritual dance festival.

Near the city periphery of Tucson begins the Saguaro National Park, named after the sometimes ten-meter-high cacti which stand in the desert landscape like outsize candlesticks. Naturally, we drove out into the desert several times, which was just beginning to bloom with almost incredible beauty, and of course we made contact with the treacherous dangers of the wilderness, which at first we had not taken seriously. There are, for instance, the prickly bushes which "shoot" at anyone who comes near. I learned this drastic lesson myself. In the evening I had to pull the barbs of these "shots" from the calves of my legs. A painful process.

Our next goal: Albuquerque. Jacqueline Denissoff, who was expecting to meet us at the airport, missed us — or we missed her. In any case, we had to take a taxi to the guesthouse of the University of New Mexico, which again we could only reach with difficulty because the whole campus was full of groups who, gathered around the innumerable loud-speakers, were listening to Robert Kennedy making an election speech against the extremely colorful backdrop of an open-air stage. Quite apart from my lectures not only in Albuquerque but also in Santa Fe, we did much else — trips to the villages of the Pueblos in the desert where the *mesas* inhabited by the Indians stood up like giant stumps of trees; a car trip to Los Alamos, the once forbidden but now accessible town in which the first atom bomb was invented. But all of that was overshadowed on our last evening in Albuquerque by an event which shook the United States to its very foundations. On the journey from Jacqueline's home to the motel situated on the edge of the city, our driver, a young Jesuit, told us that he had just heard on the radio the news that Martin Luther King had been shot. While I was changing for my lecture I heard our companion, who had followed me without ceremony into my room, keep on groaning loudly ("My God, how awful!" "What is going to happen now?"). The lecture and discussion were held as normal; not a word about the dreadful event. But we did sit in front of the television in our room long into the night and heard the famous speech of the murdered man: "I have a dream ..." as well as an endless series of interviews. But right up to the point where, the next afternoon, we took our leave of Jacqueline and her family at the airport, nothing unusual was to be seen in the city or heard in conversation. People remained silent and seemed to be paralyzed. Then, as we were driving with the airport bus into the city of St. Louis in the gathering dusk, we noticed that the city center was almost empty of people, but we thought no more about it. But when during the evening meal in the hotel restaurant we asked the waiter whether we were in the business area of the city and whether it was worthwhile taking a look around, he raised his hands in warning: "Stay inside! Myself, I live out of town, and I wish I were home already!" Naturally we did go out into the street, which by now was dark; there was literally not a single person to be seen. But then along came a crowd of clearly aggressive black youths, and we turned quickly back into the hotel. The next day, on the sight-seeing tour, there was again no sign of unrest. In the evening, following an arrangement made by telephone from New Mexico, we met with two Catholic priests from whom we were told we could expect very concrete information about the situation of the black population. And so we took a taxi to the restaurant which, on the previous evening, our waiter said with a dubious shake of the head bordered closely on a really bad neighborhood. By this, of course, he meant the black quarter. While we were having a drink at the bar two men in bright grey pullovers came up to either side of us. They introduced themselves as parish priest and curate. At the evening meal to which we were invited, we came straight to the point. They both had the task of renovating dilapidated houses with public funds from Washington. They were then handed over to the needy — not simply as a gift, but I can't remember under what especially favorable conditions. "So, you have a parish in the black quarter?" "No, we just live in a house there. And the church is beside it." At first I did not quite understand the answer. But naturally the important thing was the information. So it was new to us to find that the blacks not only did not have a spirit of solidarity between themselves like the Chinese, but they also had no sense of family. Strictly speaking there were no families — at the most, women with children who did not necessarily have the same father. This was inherited from the time of slavery in which marriage was impossible. After the meal we drove in the darkness into the middle of the black quarter. On the main street, along which on the following day — which President Johnson had declared a National Day of Mourning — a silent march would be held, most of the shops were protected by wooden or iron shutters; both our escorts feared there would be trouble, certainly for the day after next, the burial day of the murdered man, which had been claimed by the blacks as their special and real day of mourning. "But don't imagine that the plundering and destruction here will be completely unplanned." The parish priest pointed to particular shop windows as we drove by. "In there are the books where debts are recorded; and these children believe that when the books are burnt the debts are gone."

We finally stopped in front of a house that had just been handed over to a black "family." We only met the "father," who was working at covering the walls of a room with dreadful plastic paneling. He was being helped silently by a white man of whom the parish priest said — without introducing us — he must be a Jesuit lay-brother not well known to him. It was obviously much more

63

important to him to say in a loud voice that the decoration of the living room was "great," absolutely wonderful. Meantime, we went without ceremony through the whole apartment and observed almost in horror the indescribable disarray: in the bedroom a push-bike was leaning against a grimy pillow on the rumpled bedclothes. On the handle-bars of the bike hung a pair of socks; on top of the TV two plates with half eaten food; in the kitchen a pile of heaped-up dishes with half-dried food on them — and so on. We made no comment, while the two clerics observed us with obvious amusement. The floor above, which was rented to a female student, was nicely furnished and absolutely clean. On the corridor there was a Sacred Heart oil print with under it the words: "Celebrate your existence!" In the meantime a second black man had come into the house. He earnestly asked us also to look at his apartment nearby, which he had acquired in the same process. On the way there he told us about it enthusiastically, and then his two benefactors were also full of praise, although the sight was just as devastating as the previous one. As we returned to the car I asked where the women and children were. The astonishing answer was: "Don't ask too many questions!" But that did not stop me from asking about the pastoral work of the two priests. They answered rather tersely that the first thing to do was to awaken a sense of responsibility, and to settle the "father" in the house and in the family. To speak of baptism, sacraments and Mass before that would be of no avail. "Later they will come of themselves." In the meantime we had arrived at the "parish house," where all we could see was a confined office space. They called an enormous dog, patted him, and put him in the car. For the sake of comparison we were now to visit a white family which had found itself in the same straits as the black ones and which had been assigned a renovated house under the same help program. On the way there we came past a small park. It was already ten o'clock in the evening. The parish priest stopped the car for a moment: "Look, if we were in Italy there would be music,

64

people would be strolling up and down, they would be singing and flirting and dancing. And in St. Louis? No one would go into a park after dark! That's how it is in America."

Despite the late hour, we went unannounced into the midst of a family of five who were sitting in front of a TV screen in a completely normal, well-furnished living room. The housewife gave us a friendly greeting and asked if we would like something to drink. But our two clerics did not want to stay long; as if they were at home there, they took us through the apartment; the kitchen seemed to them to be especially worth seeing, and it was indeed sparkling and clean; the extractor fan above the stove was pointed out to us. A quarter of an hour later we were already on our way back to the hotel. "For this beautiful kitchen," we were told, "the people received less money than our blacks. But when a black man goes into the city to buy an extractor fan like that, on the way he will see, let's say, an especially fine TV set on display – and so he buys it, although he doesn't need it. But the money for the kitchen is gone. After a while, the parish priest added: "The crucial difference is the difference in *background*." (This term means a variety of things: cultural tradition; the milieu that shapes and makes demands on people; education; and perhaps other things as well.) When I referred to the number of highly educated black people in the medical and legal professions I was answered with a laugh, but quite definitely: "None of us would ever go to a black doctor or lawyer!" To this day the answer of these two priests, who were dedicating their lives to the service of the black people, has remained incomprehensible to me.

We spent a restless night watching TV reports about looting, riots, and arson in the big cities —above all, Chicago — and then attended a Palm Sunday Mass in the Old Cathedral of St. Louis. Then, curious and worried, we flew out to this very Chicago where several universities had invited me to lecture. During the journey to the hotel we saw, as yet, nothing unsettling. On the bed in the hotel we found a card, conspicuously placed, asking us to double-lock the room even (and especially?) while we were occupying it. This seemed to be completely normal here. But then came a phone call from De Paul University to say that my lecture planned for that evening was to be postponed to the next morning, because a curfew for all students under twenty-one made their attendance at the lecture impossible. There was also a message from Loyola University. They preferred to keep to the evening arrangement for the following day, but the lecture would take place to a small audience.

During our first evening walk we had the impression of being in an enemy-occupied city. In the grassy area of Michigan Avenue there were military bivouacs. In front of the tents the weapons were stacked in pyramids. Jeeps, with soldiers wearing steel helmets and clutching weapons between their knees, were continually driving by. Fifty thousand men, we heard, along with police and the National Guard, were deployed throughout the country. On the other hand, as was to be expected, life went on. Not even the Ice Review in the Boulevard Room of the Hilton Hotel was canceled. I did not want to deny it to my son after I had, in 1950, been absolutely astonished to see how, a few minutes before the start, the dance floor was lowered and disappeared sideways under the floor, and the ice surface rose. The swirling show began immediately while the spectators at the same time enjoyed their dinner. Next day as we were crouched in front of the television, we heard, with feelings of shame, the report at the funeral of Martin Luther King of his friend Ralph Abernathy — whom I had got to know at a teach-in at the University of Toronto — how, each time they were to go off to prison again, they fasted for twenty-four hours to purify their spirits and to prevent hatred from arising in them towards their judges and prison wardens.

I had in these days often enough felt myself in a completely paradoxical and exceptional situation. For example, one was not prepared, when invited to a banquet on the twenty-fourth story of a high-rise building, to see out the window, over whole sections of the city, the night sky lit up by two or three enormous fires which clearly no one was dealing with. And yet all of that was continually sidelined by the friendly, direct human encounters which we experienced, precisely here in Chicago.

One of my Stanford students, who, after twelve years was now an Assistant Professor at the Northwestern University some kilometers away from Chicago, brought us to Erich Heller, who had emigrated to Germany, and who had now invited me to give a lecture in German on the theme "Abuse of Language — Abuse of Power." In his office we had, beforehand, a very lively and elated conversation over a glass of wine. By chance I discovered on his bookshelves the volume of letters which Peter Suhrkamp, one of the numerous friends we had in common, had written to his authors after the war. "You do know that the earliest letter he wrote, the earliest in the series, was written to you?" I had forgotten; but now Heller took hold of the book to prove it to me, and then he read out the date: 26 November 1945!

On Holy Thursday we made our way to the Benedictine Monastery in Minnesota which then dashed our hopes of a really festive Easter celebration. During the Easter Mass it was already beginning to snow. The coldest city in the United States is to be found in the state of Minnesota. The bus that brought us on Easter Monday to the airport in St. Paul had a thick layer of snow on the roof. In Chicago, from where we started our non-stop flight to New Orleans, we could see as we took off over the city that there was still smoke from some fires. And as we were leaving the plane on landing we thought we had walked into the exhaust heat from the engines; but this was the normal temperature of the Mississippi Delta, and there was air-conditioning in the bus that took us to the reception area, so that it was possible to breathe again.

The Roosevelt Hotel, a somewhat old-fashioned and pompous

caravansary housing the Philosophers Congress, had set up a brightly colored enclosure in the lobby, in which, as Easter Bunnies, a few dozen rabbits were romping about.

The first thing that had to be seen in New Orleans was the Old Man River which, with its brown water and broad as an estuary, flowed by the city. Then a stroll through the French Quarter, in which there were innumerable night clubs with doors opening wide onto the street and where more or less naked dancers plied their trade. – In his words of welcome to the Congress, the Archbishop of New Orleans probably had the French Quarter in mind as he reassured us that in this city – unlike in New York or Chicago — it was possible to walk through the streets in the dark without fear of being mugged; here there was "much sin, but little crime." I was told that the Archbishop had been a military chaplain with a parachute regiment. In general, he seemed optimistic. He thought, for example, that New Orleans, because of the charming way people dealt with one another — under the French influence — could serve as a model for the general interrelationships between the races. I asked a colleague from Chicago, who I knew had grown up in New Orleans, what he thought of the Archbishop's judgment about the race problem. He put his black spectacle case up in front of his eyes and said he did not wear glasses like that!

When the conferring of the Aquinas Medal in the Grand Ball Room of the hotel was completed with solemn ceremony, in my response I spoke, in line with the general theme of the Congress – "The Future" — about the possible future of philosophy. My conclusion was that perhaps under the reign of sophistry and pseudo-philosophy true philosophy as a distinguishable independent discipline would disappear, and the specifically philosophical object — the root of things and the ultimate meaning of existence — would only be considered by those with *faith*. Despite the friendly applause I was somewhat doubtful whether my American colleagues agreed with this prognosis. Amongst those congratulating me —

my son first — I was surprised to see my Japanese translator and former travel companion who, in the meantime, had become a Professor of the State University of Kyushu in Fukuoka and was now in Washington for a year as guest lecturer. His wife also appeared, dressed in a kimono and with a baby on her arm. Her contribution to the conversation was limited to a charmingly shy smile; she probably had not a word of English. I had to think of the time when in Nagoya five years previously she greeted me in her house, with her head bowed down to the floor, and then, kneeling, served both of us men at table. Naturally, for herself and her husband it would have been unthinkable for her now to go out with us, and so my Japanese friend and Michael and I went to a French restaurant to celebrate with Californian red wine our reunion and the festive occasion. The style was very un-American. Anyone not wearing a jacket and tie would not be admitted. When a flambéed dish was being brought in and served, a bell was sounded, the lights were put out and the waiter sang a French song.

I was, above all, interested in finding out what might possibly have changed in this city of New Orleans — which I was now visiting for the third time — since the legislation was introduced outlawing racial segregation and since the murder of Martin Luther King. Riots and arson had not occurred here, which was surprising. And so I rang, as I had also done in 1950 and 1956, the "white" priest at Corpus Christi, the largest black parish in the United States, to arrange for a conversation with him. He was not available but arranged for us to meet another likewise "white" priest the following day at Peter Claver House where the National Urban League had its office — a nation-wide organization of black people. He would introduce us there and we would receive much more authentic information than he could give us himself. The taxi driver almost went on strike when he heard where we wanted him to drive us. For us it was again quite instructive to hear, for half an hour, the blunt comments of the "man in the street" — the white man, at least — and what he thought of the "niggers." "One, by himself, looks like an angel; but two or three together are a mob." Again and again he would say as we drove by a black man: "Does he look like someone looking for work? But he is paid for by our government!" — and so on.

In Peter Claver House, a rather battered-looking three-story building, we were expected. A good-looking young black woman in an elegant, brightly colored suit, seemingly an academic, told us that the priest we were to meet was running late, but that she was happy to give us information. "So, ask away!" This was said in a tone which, while polite, suggested she was argumentative. That suited me fine. I told her about my first visit to New Orleans, in 1950, and praised the noticeable progress: black and white people were now naturally together both in buses and restaurants as if it had always been like that. But our stern lady would not hear of it. "The reality is that there is absolutely no progress!" "How is there not?" "Because nothing has changed in the racism of the whites." "But perhaps something has changed in the blacks — since the murder of Martin Luther King?" — "Yes, that's true. If someone hits me today, I hit back. Martin Luther King — I belonged to his inner circle — forbade us to do that. But his famous 'dream' cannot be realized. In any case, I don't believe in it anymore!" She was becoming, in the meantime, more and more curt and aggressive. The whole thing was like a duel. I reminded her quietly of the deceased Archbishop of New Orleans who had excommunicated three prominent Catholics of the city for their propaganda in favor of racial segregation; perhaps the attitude of the Catholic Church was a special case? "No, not at all special! The Archbishop was completely isolated; his own clergy opposed him!" "And how do you see the prospects for the future?" "The future? One day, without any need for legislation, we will in fact be living in reservations just like the Indians! The whites, with their shopping centres and golf courses are simply moving away!" In the meantime, the priest

70

we were to meet had come in unnoticed; he listened to us for a while in silence. He found our dramatic debate interesting, if not altogether amusing. I told him briefly all I had heard. To my surprise, he agreed with it all entirely, even with what the aggressive lady said about the attitude of the Catholic clergy. The conversation continued for a while longer. Then this man, who was undoubtedly conversant with the situation, said very seriously: "You know, something new has happened recently: the black people themselves no longer want this much talked-about integration. You asked about the future. I can only say that there is no solution in sight." Depressed, we took our leave. And after we eventually found a taxi, obviously a rare thing in this neighborhood, we drove in silence back to the hotel.

Next day departure for Washington. The hypermodern airport built by the Finnish architect Saarinen is fifty kilometers outside the city. The chatty taxi driver told us about the turmoil and destruction of the previous week. To our question whether that had all been planned he gave us the puzzling answer: "Naturally! It was just done a bit earlier." Meanwhile we were driving, as evening closed in, through the park landscape. Through the emerging green of the trees the white flowering dogwood shrubs were gleaming. And then the dome of the Capitol suddenly appeared. — In the following days, while I carried out my lecturing duties my son visited the sights of the capital city.

After a morning colloquium I asked a friendly colleague, a priest, to accompany me to a bank to vouch for me as I cashed the checks I had gathered in the meantime as honoraria for my lectures. I was surprised that they brought the dollar notes up from the cellar. My companion, for his part surprised by my naivety, answered: "You think a bank would have even one hundred dollar note lying on the counter?" And then he told me about a friend who had been attacked and robbed here in the middle of Washington. "They jump on you from behind, hold your mouth closed, and go for your wallet. And you let them take it, otherwise out comes the knife."

The next day we visited — since we could hardly leave it out — the National Shrine, which was built at a cost of thirty million dollars. It is dedicated to the Immaculate Conception. It is an outsize imitation, built with the most expensive materials, of all the Marian shrines in the world – from Guadeloupe to Fatima and Lourdes. Whenever we mentioned the National Shrine there was no one who was not embarrassed.

On our last day in Washington a relatively young colleague collected us and our luggage from the hotel. We were all packed and ready for departure. He took us for a slow drive through some of the streets — now lit up in broad daylight — which had been ravaged by riots and plundering. There was hardly anyone to be seen. On individual walls of houses the words "Soul Brother" were written in simple handwriting as a plea to be left alone. But that hadn't helped. The devastation zone ended only five blocks short of the White House.

We were invited for midday dinner to a young professor's small family who lived in a terraced house a few hundred meters from the Capitol. At table German was spoken; the mother was Austrian, and they used to spend the long vacation in Munich. "Every time, when coming from a concert or the theater in a German city we have to become accustomed again to walking home through the streets without being molested. In Washington, where there is sometimes glorious music to be heard, you go together in tight groups to the parking place and drive home in a car that is locked from the inside." And naturally the conversation came around to the terrifying nights of upheaval. "We didn't go to bed at all. We spent the night waiting, with our cases packed. We knew that no one would help us. The police were instructed not to intervene."

In New York there would be no more lecturing engagements;

the last week was to be devoted to theater, musicals, art collections — but also to some meetings with publishers, which, of course, were becoming ever more difficult. We were not ready for a meeting right at the end which would change Michael's travel plans and have us return home with especially good memories. We had hardly arrived in the hotel I was familiar with near St. Patrick's Cathedral when I telephoned Helen Wolff who had returned to New York after the death of her husband. She immediately invited us to dinner in a Chinese restaurant. It was situated quite close to her little apartment and her publishing house office. We reminded one another of the time long ago when she lived in Washington Square, then still an almost idyllic place, where at the beginning of the 50's I had myself often observed men silently playing the royal game of chess on stone tables, surrounded by spectators. "Those times are long gone when, without worrying, you could let children play on the square." Then followed a series of true stories, all dealing with the one main topic: the continually increasing insecurity. For instance, the shop assistant in a fish shop, who was able to give her expert advice, confided to her that he was "really" a teacher, but that, although he loved the profession, had one day given it up out of fear of the pupils. You could never turn your back on them. He had been through the whole Korean War; but to teach in a trade school — his nerves were not strong enough for that; it was better to be selling fish.

In America, especially in New York — according to Helen Wolff — there were problems which were simply unknown to us in Germany, at least at this level of severity. For instance, all at once eight hundred thousand Puerto Ricans had come into the city of New York because it had the highest level of social security. A good number did get work; and then it emerged that for an at-first surprising reason their situation was not completely hopeless: in contrast to the blacks, who are always completely isolated individuals, for the Puerto Ricans there are traditional, ordered social structures propped up by the authorities. If, for example, in a factory a fight with knives breaks out between Puerto Ricans, the manager turns to the priest who has come with them as a migrant, and order is then successfully restored. — After arranging another visit to the publishing firm we accompanied our hostess to her house door. We were, after all, in New York.

I would almost have forgotten that I had another lecture appointment: at the University of Syracuse in New York State. The spontaneous memory that went through my mind of the adventurous trip to Syracuse in Sicily with my son Thomas was suddenly erased by the journey through the American industrial city. The mostly young male and female lecturers did think up something adventurous: before the lecture there was a dinner in Wild West style. We walked over sawdust through the room, which was dimly lit with petroleum lamps, to a table made of rough-hewn boards. Earthenware jugs were then placed on the table, and on them, written in chalk, you could read the menu and the wine list. The wine, originating not far from Syracuse, was surprisingly good; and as for the steak, the pride of the house, you could eat only one third of it. In good spirits, the diners were not sparing with the wine and the conversation became increasingly lively, with a certain perkiness bordering on frivolity — although the subject under discussion was "the new liturgy." A young female lecturer spoke about a Mass at which a nun danced a bit too sexily for her taste. A Jesuit, not recognizable as a priest, made a case for including films in the celebration of Mass. I told them about a jazz vesper in New York about which my son and I had had an argument. In reply, someone said that in his dictionary of American slang the word "jazz" originally referred to the sex act.

After my lecture, held this time without a written text — unusually for me — and probably a bit more lively, another sort of party was organized at which I had to argue endlessly with a particularly insistent man who was the "Death of God" theologian most discussed in the media. I had been forewarned about him, unfortunately in vain. — Dead tired after all of this, I slept so soundly that I almost missed the flight to New York.

But I arrived at the appointed time to meet Helen Wolff who looks after the "Helen and Kurt Wolff Books" section of the gigantic publishing house Harcourt, Brace and World. A manuscript of Georges Simenon happened to be on her desk. I was interested in the author because of his unusual way of working which I had found out about by chance from his own account: for weeks he would think out a situation which forces the characters to make an extreme decision; and then he would write it down within, I think, eleven days. Helen Wolff passed the original (typed, by the way) manuscript to me across the table, and I saw something that I was well acquainted with from my methods: nothing but the crossing out of superfluous words.

For my own book we agreed on a volume with various essays on Plato. But it soon became clear that nothing would come of it — just like the agreement concluded on the same day with Herder and Herder to publish my TV plays.

The next day a bunch of flowers was sent to me to my hotel room announcing the arrival of a friend. This was particularly significant. When our son Thomas collapsed in July 1964 on Mount Rainier at the White River Camp a doctor was found who took charge of him while he was already nearly on the point of dying. He accompanied him in a Park Ranger's car, which was modified to serve as an ambulance, to a small hospital on the way to Seattle. But naturally my son's companions traveling with him had, in their total surprise, not made a note of the doctor's name. But I was keen to find him to thank him for his unselfish help. So I went to the administration of the camp site not knowing the name. Soon I received a very sympathetic letter from there, in which the ranger, probably a simple type of man, not only told me the name and address of the doctor and described in detail the series of events of that evening, but also added that he had often been told that the landscape there was reminiscent of the German alps and that we might be consoled to think that our son might well almost have felt at home on Mount Rainier.

The doctor, who had pitched his own tent at the camp site, came from Vinalhaven in the US State of Maine — at the other end of the continent. Naturally I wrote to him immediately — and received the astonishing answer that he had long since had my address from the chancellery of Berkeley University but had hesitated to contact me. Now he wanted to say to me that a part of himself traveled that night to Seattle. We exchanged a few more letters, and finally an invitation to Vinalhaven arrived. That there is an American city called Augusta was news to me, but that is the name of the capital city of Maine State in the north-east of the United States. I landed there in September 1967 on the way to Canada. The doctor was expecting me — a lively man, ten to fifteen years younger than me. In his big car we drove immediately to the coast. Vinalhaven is an island. Dinner in a fine old-fashioned guest-house which was once the home of the author of *Uncle Tom's Cabin*. My host, as he later confessed, had scruples about asking the author of "Discipline and Moderation" [Zucht und Mass] whether he would fancy a drink before the meal. But then he was both surprised and relieved when I asked for a Bloody Mary which he had as yet never heard of. And then he joyfully ordered also a bottle of Château-Neuf-du-Pape. Early next morning a ferry brought us onto Vinalhaven. The bottles and glass spheres floating on the water indicated the presence of the lobster pots laid out under them by the fishermen. Lobsters are the special delicacy on the island. I was to have them served to me in many different forms. Vinalhaven had only twelve hundred inhabitants. My friend was the only doctor on the island. In my room I found a framed photo of Thomas on the wall. He said he had taken to Thomas immediately; he also thought him much younger than he really was.

76

He was moved as he recalled once again the details of that death journey at night. After two days, during which time we had become good friends, we bade farewell to one another.

And so now he had come to New York not only to see me but also Thomas's brother. We did not have to think long and hard about what to do together. Instead, we found ourselves confronted with a perfect program: it had been generously and inventively thought out. Already on the first evening, in an expensive restaurant at a table reserved for four people, we were introduced to a prominent black singer. Planned for the next evening was a visit to a witty and audacious musical we had missed. Played at a fierce tempo, it was a transposition — with slight homoerotic overtones — of Shakespeare's *As You Like It*. The doctor had seen it weeks earlier to judge whether it would be suitable for us to see, and only then did he order the tickets. Then, quite unexpectedly came the invitation to Michael to go to Vinalhaven for a few days. The two of them were getting on well together, and the trip was quickly arranged. Within a quarter of an hour the flight tickets were changed.

For me, after just six weeks my journey to receive the Aquinas Medal was over; in the meantime, at the university in Münster the Summer Semester 1968 had already begun. In pouring rain the doctor brought me and my luggage to the bus terminal. As we parted company we did not know we would not see one another again. Death had brought us together and, only a few years later, death would also separate us.

IV
The Walnut Tree and the Birch

One of the letters awaiting me on my return from what was supposed to be my last trip to America contained news of the death of the poet George von der Vring. I had not heard from him for many years, and had hardly ever thought of him anymore. But this news of his death refreshed my memory of an almost forgotten story going back more than thirty years. It had to do with the birth of our son Thomas whose place of work in Berkeley University we had visited only a few weeks previously.

In the first volume of my memoirs I described how in the summer of 1936 I had cycled with my younger brother down to South Germany and visited Albrecht Goes in his village presbytery near Ulm. Thinking to promote my early writings about courage and hope in the "Eckart" journal, the reviewer, Albrecht Goes, who was completely unknown to me at the time, had sought information about me from the publisher Hegner in Leipzig. When the publisher had passed on this request to me, I had sent a few lines in reply — in an unduly abrupt, typically Westphalian style — to this inquisitive Swabian. Some decades later he had sent back this postcard — which he had kept as a kind of curiosity — attached to a friendly letter of birthday greeting. Our first personal meeting did indeed become "friendship at first sight." It was especially difficult to stop naming and praising to one another our favorite poems, and, as it turned out, for the most part they were the same for both of us. One poem, in particular, came to mind, which I hesitated to mention. I thought it might perhaps not be good enough for my knowledgeable and critical host to include it in his private anthology. I said that to him and added, almost apologetically, that for my wife, at least, since the birth of our son Thomas these verses had taken on a special significance. But when I then named the poet, Georg von der Vring, and the title of the poem "The Walnut Tree," Albrecht Goes banged his hand on the table: "I know this poem really well!" He also knew the poet well. He lived in Stuttgart. He had written the poem down in one sitting when, after a long wait, his son was born; and "by chance" a certain young priest — himself, namely — baptized the boy. Naturally I knew the poem by heart, and as I recited it Albrecht Goes said some lines with me, the last one with great assurance:

When your mother gave birth to you
A tree rustled and prophesied.
A walnut tree out there beside the window
Moved its leafy hand.
It put down beside your little body
Three shiny walnuts. All ripe.
And so in this rich moment
Your little mouth opened in song.

I had read this poem to my wife a few weeks before the birth of our first child, and immediately she took possession of it as something which quite obviously applied to herself. Secretly she learned it by heart. After unexpectedly long and painful labor pains, Thomas came into the world; and during those difficult days — and, above all, at night — she had, as I was told later, recited these lines to herself when she was alone; the midwife had kept on running out so as not to miss the boxing match being relayed by radio from New York between Max Schmeling and the as yet undefeated Joe Louis. She kept coming back excitedly and reporting. Only once did I use such an absence to look through the half-open door and snatch a look, in helpless sympathy, at my beloved wife as she suffered. She admitted to me only years later how awful it had been. In the meantime, the customs and the wishes in this respect have changed radically in a way that is difficult for my generation to understand. Our grandchildren have all seen the light of day in the presence of their father.

On that unforgettable summer afternoon, Albrecht Goes suggested writing a letter to our friend Georg von der Vring to tell him about our unusual meeting. In a postscript I added the question whether I might ask of the poet a hand-written copy of the Walnut Tree poem for my wife. When I arrived back home there was a letter from Georg von der Vring on the table with the hand-written poem.

Now the poet, almost seventy-nine years old, had died on 1 March 1968. His contemporaries had almost forgotten him, although years before the successful war books of Erich Maria Remarque and Ludwig Renn he had published his novel *The Soldier Suhren* [Soldat Suhren], the first artistically important report arising out of the World War I. From the comprehensive obituary, in which Wilhelm E. Süskind convincingly celebrated him as "the most poetic and for that reason the most indispensable of German lyric poets" of the last decades, I discovered the shocking, never explained fact that the body of Georg von der Vring was retrieved from the Isar by sappers during a training exercise. His face looked, according to the report of some friends, spirited and defiant. That is exactly as I remember him from the one meeting we had. It was probably in the late '50s. I was to give a lecture in Newman House in Munich. In those days, the lecture halls were full. Extra chairs were brought in. I stood waiting in the corridor and Georg von der Vring surprisingly came up to me, gave me his name, took my hand, and spoke with great urgency. His expression was "spirited and defiant," but also somewhat tormented. But in the unrest surrounding us his words were virtually unintelligible. Then he took his leave. Unexpectedly quick and sudden. But he did not go into the hall — perhaps he was repelled by the crowd. Perhaps he had just wanted to greet me. I was somewhat bemused as I watched him leave.

As I write this now during the week of Pentecost 1987, they are all gone: the poet, my son — who at birth had indeed received the gift of song — and also the mother who bore him. But I have not been able to find the hand-written Walnut Tree poem in her papers; probably she had kept the page only too safe.

In the same volume "Jahresring," which the culture circle of the Federal Association of German Industry produces every year, to my surprise I came across a second, unusually comprehensive obituary, likewise dedicated to a poet who had died in 1968 and by whom another of my favorite poems was written. When I was sixteen I had written it into a blue school copybook along with some poems of lesser quality; I can't remember where I had found it. When I then saw it by chance more than twenty years later, it seemed to me such an unusual poem that it became the only poem which I have attempted to interpret in a published essay. In the days when violence reigned I deliberately suppressed the name of the poet and even pretended I did not know it. As a result of this and other circumstances some confusion later arose which is now long forgotten. But the lines, and also the poet, whom, not without success, I had forced into anonymity, are not to be forgotten — if I can help it. In a story I invented I had some friends and, above all, a rather mysterious woman, praise the poem, which read as follows:

Delicate birch tree, bow down
Deep into the sky,
The evening star enters
Your hanging branches

In its tender surrounds
It shines doubly clear,
A fish in the heavenly weir,
Golden and wonderful.

In this form the poem came to the attention of readers of the *Frankfurter Zeitung* in November 1942. It was, in fact, not given in its entirety; only the first two verses were printed. Obviously — and that is how I see it today — the author was not able to sustain right to the end the precision of the beginning, which was as if drawn with a silver pen. What I thought was special about this poem was that the sky was not seen as high, but low, and that the birch tree was to bow down to it. This was completed through seeing the evening star as the fish in the weir, producing the image of a world sunk into night as into the sea. As the young woman in my story formulated it in her calm, dark voice: despite definition that was as clear as day, the underground flow and mystery of the watery element was everywhere present.

After a short time the editors sent me some letters from their readers communicating to the author, who supposedly did not know it, not only the name of the author but also the complete text of the poem. Obviously my essay had brought the largely forgotten poem back to the attention of readers who must have already known it. And so I was told that Theodor Abele, editor of the fine anthology "Der Kranz," was wondering whether he should include it the next edition of the book. — A university lecturer described my overall interpretation as the product of unacceptably mystifying subtlety and put forward his own interpretation; but the editors said they had no intention of publishing it. As against that — as I found out later from a friend who was one of the editors — they were looking at the suggestion that I should be entrusted generally with reviewing books of poetry. But then, for better or for worse, nothing came of it: in May 1943 — just a few months after my essay was published — the *Frankfurter Zeitung* was suppressed by Hitler.

My unwillingness to name the poet had to do with this wretched regime. Because of early anti-war poems, Wilhelm Klemm had come under suspicion with the authorities. The rumor was circulating that he was excluded from the Chamber of Professional Writers [Reichsschriftumskammer], and so I did not want to draw attention to him by mentioning his name publicly. Perhaps he was in prison? Of course, Wilhelm Klemm was himself, strangely, not entirely innocent regarding his almost total disappearance from public awareness. For decades he had published no more poems. In *Kürschners Literatur-Kalender* his name was simply not included; and in a literary work about the history of expressionism which appeared after World War II and which made claims to completeness, it was said that Wilhelm Klemm died in 1945. He hated giving information about himself. Kurt Pinthus said in his obituary that he had once asked Wilhelm Klemm for some autobiographical information for the documentary volume *Menschheitsdämmerung*, which had first appeared in 1923, was reprinted several times, and again finally in 1967. The complete information he received was: "Born in Leipzig, living there."

In reality Wilhelm Klemm, despite being under a cloud and being hampered by the authorities, had led a very active life, not as a poet, of course, but as a highly successful publisher. Not only, after the death of Alfred Kröner, did he become director of the publishing house founded by Kröner which was known for the blue volumes of the "Paperback Edition," but on his own initiative he also published the superbly presented four volumes of the "Dieterich Collection." It was only in 1960 that I found out about all of this and about his move to Wiesbaden. At one of the Poets' Evenings with the student teachers in Essen the lines from the "Delicate Birch Tree," along with my interpretation, were discussed in detail. And now we wanted to find out the opinion of

the poet whom everyone thought was dead but who was now unexpectedly contactable. So I sent him my essay, which had been
first published almost twenty years ago. By now eighty years old,
he spontaneously wrote me a letter, several pages long, in expansive
handwriting, saying that he had not looked at the poem himself as
closely as that; he had even — *horribile dictu* — not thought much
of it; and now his "eyes were opened" by others. Especially what
"the lady" [Freundin] said about the fish in the weir and about the
water he found "very apt and surprising." He had written the poem
"at one short sitting … without effort and without much deliber-
ation."

It surprised me that in the letter there was no mention, one
way or the other, that my interpretation had simply ignored the
second half of the poem.

This really inappropriate halving of the poem has been largely
followed, and, unbelievably, my intentionally false claim that I did
not know who the author was has also been taken at face value and
accepted as historical fact. At any rate, in a German reader meant
for school use only the first two stanzas are included — with the
addition that the identity of the poet is "unknown."

V

Santa Fe and Escorial

There is a special reason why both names are closely linked in my memory. In both places, even in Spain, it was exclusively Americans, all of them Catholic Christians, who invited me to give a series of lectures. One place was Santa Fe, the capital of New Mexico State, in a Seminary where at the time only the Dean and the Spiritual Director were in residence. The other place was the University of Maria Cristina, likewise empty of students because of the summer holidays. A raised walkway across the street led from the university to the Escorial, the gigantic complex which Philip II erected on the high plain of Castile as monastery, regal palace, and mausoleum. And strangely, the same reasoning was used by both groups — which, by the way, knew nothing of one another, and lived in regions of the world separated by thousands of kilometers. Some maintained that America radiated nothing visibly Christian; that was why they were going to Spain. The others, in New Mexico, maintained that for three hundred years Mass had been celebrated daily; here the Catholic tradition, even when it was hidden and suppressed, was still more effective and present than anywhere else in America.

Of course, in America there is no building to compare with the Escorial. And even in New Mexico there is no city comparable to Toledo or Avila. And certainly on the North American continent and in any other European country apart from Spain, a monument like the "Valley of the Fallen" would be inconceivable — this highly respectable and, in its conception, admirable memorial which the Franco regime had erected in honor of itself. I know that this "valley," the full name of which is Santa Cruz del Valle de los Caidos, is referred to by many a democratic-minded person — also by some of my friends — as an "accursed place." And from a purely formal point of view, it is clearly a case of the architecture reflecting power in the totalitarian style found in Mao's China, in Stalin's sphere of political influence, or in Albert Speer's plans for Hitler's empire. At the same time, the purely technical achievement, which took decades to complete and was hardly noticed by the world at large, is unparalleled in the rest of Europe: a whole, mighty granite mountain was hollowed out and the inside of it became a cathedral capable of holding several thousand people. Its dome, reminiscent of St. Peter's in Rome, reaches, at its tip, to the summit of the mountain and breaks through it. More crucial than the technical perfection is, I think, the idea which it embodies. Whatever about the political intent, it is still a magnificent idea conceived in the spirit of reconciliation: here, under a cross which dominates the landscape far and wide, all who were killed in the civil war, on whatever side they had fought, were to be interred — close to the Madonna statues indigenous to Spain and under the protection of the Benedictine monks, who every morning celebrated High Mass with choir boys from their international school. When, during my first visit, I heard the procession of choir boys preceding the monks into the Choir area begin — as if without warning — to sing "Requiem aeternam" in the Gregorian Chant I had not heard in the ten years since the Requiem Mass for our son Thomas, suddenly all kinds of political issues were forgotten and done away with.

The Escorial lies more than a thousand meters above sea level. This is where, in the summer, the prosperous people of Madrid come to relax. In this wonderfully gentle, but at the same time almost tropical warmth, the ten or twelve days could have been a refreshing time for me, too — even without the swimming pool and the high ball-playing area at the front wall, against which a Cuban Anselm specialist and I almost every morning hit a tennis ball in a game we gave the false name of "pelota." We made up our own rules of the game and played until, fairly weary, we dragged ourselves up the steps into the park to refresh ourselves in the cool water.

I have seldom found myself so suddenly put into a group of such colorful people. While swimming we constantly encountered a particularly charming couple: a young Vietnam War veteran with his beautiful red-haired wife Sharon. It was the first time I had heard this name, but he insisted it came from the Old Testament. The "veteran" seemed more like an active officer on leave from the front. We quickly became engaged in a lively conversation, and naturally I could not hear enough from this "leather-neck" with the "green beret." In the newspapers at the time there was talk of a massacre committed in a village by American soldiers on women and children. "Did such things really happen?" My "veteran" answered by telling a story followed by a question which left me bewildered. "In a village in the middle of the jungle a young woman carrying a child approached my group smiling and apparently about to ask for something. But suddenly she pulled a pistol from under the child and shot down one of the group. What do you do when, a second time, a young woman carrying a child approaches you smiling?"

On the day of my arrival I was brought into the inner courtyard with gushing fountains and oleander bushes in bloom, and I joined a discussion circle where a peaceful debate was taking place. It was late afternoon, and after the rather spare meal on the airplane I was thinking, now rather hungry, of the evening meal. But in Spain, as I found to my disappointment, the evening meal was not served — even to Americans — until a few hours before midnight. Opposite me sat an Englishman called Christopher Derrick, who soon made me forget my hunger. He was wearing a dark red pullover over his naked skin and would unselfconsciously raise it a little to scratch his belly. He told me with happy casualness that he was the author — anonymous, as was the custom — of reviews of two of my books in the Literary Supplement of the London *Times*. His turn of phrase was, as I remembered very well, aimed at intriguing and provoking the reader. And now he took a mischievous delight in explaining his secret intentions, which had also not been clear to me. We happened by chance to be speaking of C. S. Lewis, and to my surprise I learned that he had lived many years in direct personal contact with this man whom I so much admired. And so I asked him why C. S. Lewis, once he "converted" from atheism to the Christian faith, did not immediately become a Catholic as one might have expected after reading his books. Derrick answered somewhat hesitantly that this was a critical point. "Do you know, this is how I see it: someone receives a letter from the tax office; oh, he thinks, I can read that tomorrow or next week. And the letter lies there quite a while without being opened. Something like that happened to the message which, as C. S. Lewis had naturally known for a long time, the Catholic Church was sending him. The letter was never opened. But who is to judge him for it?"

While I was strolling around the covered spaces which encircled the square, one of the initiators of the course suddenly called out to me from the noisy, crowded little bar and beckoned to me to come in. We had not yet made contact. We met more by chance, as is normal in America. But now I recognized in him an old acquaintance. He even maintained that more than a decade ago in his California college he had been given the task of introducing me before my lecture on leisure. In the meantime he had written a short but compact book, which I knew very well, on the "Metaphysics of Love." And although you could hardly hear yourself speaking we began a lively debate about — among other things — his thesis, which I found problematic: a "love" which has been

kindled by the "qualities" of another, their intelligence or temperament, very easily degenerates into something like prostitution.
Naturally we could come to no agreement. We were drinking good
Spanish wine; but I found the noise and cigarette smoke equally
bothersome, and I soon took myself off to the peace of the inner
courtyard.

There I met the French Jesuit Bertrand de Margerie. People
had praised his lectures on Christology; but what was most convincing about him was the personal spirituality he radiated. His
father had been his country's ambassador in West Germany, and
he spoke German without any accent. We soon came to speak
about Cardinal Daniélou, with whom, as it soon emerged, we had
both been friends. Daniélou had been found dead in the apartment
of a dancer. But my friend knew well enough to convince me that
the sensationalism of the tabloid press was pure fiction.

Furthermore, I was wondering how — and whether at all —
the conceptually and intellectually demanding lectures of de Margerie and also my own ("Hope and History," "The Situation of
Today's Philosophizer") would be received by the quite young students, both male and female. Naturally, that remained hard to
judge, and perhaps we could be deceiving ourselves. For example,
there was the pretty girl who occupied the room next to mine who,
with the door wide open, used to display a dozen of her dainty,
laced underclothes on a cord stretched across her room like a display of flags on a ship. But on my departure I was surprised to be
given, precisely by her, an amazingly well-conceived note of
thanks. Again and again you find it unbelievable how naturally and
without concern these young Americans express themselves. Could
one imagine that a German student would send me a letter like
the one that was sent on to me to the Escorial by an American student in Ohio? He said that one day, in the bookshop of his college,
with an ironic grin he had taken down my book (*Belief and Faith*)
from the shelf, saying to himself: "Let's see how it drips with

'goody-goody nonsense.' But then it was as if I had touched a high-tension wire and couldn't let go of it. In fact, I don't want to let go until I have devoured all that you have written." I am not embarrassed to confess that as an author you like reading this kind of thing.

The audience in the Escorial did not consist only of students. There were also some priests. I am grateful to one of them, a Melchitic Christian, for his unforgettable visual lesson on the theme of "Sign and Symbol," about which I thought I understood a thing or two myself. He raised his right hand and showed me how in his Eastern Church the sign of the cross is made: thumb, forefinger and middle finger, brought together as a physical sign of the Trinity, touch the forehead, breast and shoulders, while the other two fingers, representing the two natures of Christ, are placed side by side in the palm of the hand.

I was dealing exclusively with priests in Santa Fe, where, in the summer of 1970, four weeks of the most remarkable experiences awaited me. On the way there I had to spend several hours in the Dallas airport. With a certain curiosity I entered the spacious building and immediately I had to admire the fascinating trick they used to render attractive — with restaurants, bookshops, and souvenir stands — these kilometer-long walk-ways which ultimately lead to the entrance hall. In London or in Frankfurt you are oppressed by the dreary monotony. But here in Dallas the endless distance had been so cleverly divided up by the use of bright ceiling hangings which were constantly changing in form and color — in the language of the theater they are called teasers — that every few minutes you had the impression of being in a different room.

At a leisurely pace I headed for the bar and ordered myself a Bloody Mary, the only one of the eight kinds of cocktail I had been offered in the United States which I really took to and then even used to drink at home. For once, the name, which refers to the

English Queen Mary, did not disturb me. It is a strange drink; you would think you were looking at a large glass of tomato juice, and apart from the additional taste of tabasco — which could be more or less sharp, depending on the gusto of the bar-man mixing the drink — it also tasted like pure tomato juice. The first time I ordered one I asked the barman if he had not forgotten to add the shot of vodka, which is, of course, the main ingredient. He answered promptly: "Drink another glass, and then you'll have a better idea." In front of the bar in Dallas – something which made me slightly suspicious — there was a colored board displaying recipes for mixing one or two dozen cocktails. The explanation was soon clear. When, in all innocence, I ordered a Bloody Mary I was asked if I had the necessary vodka with me; here it was against the law to serve vodka or whisky. But, of course, I could buy them in any drugstore in the city. Perhaps I would like a beer? "No thanks." The thought immediately came to me that only in America could you find something so fanciful, but then I thought that "that kind of thing" could also really happen in Canada, not to speak of India. But I was then reminded of something else which had happened a few hours ago on the flight to Dallas. Probably there are not many things of which one can say that they could only happen in America and nowhere else. But what I had just experienced was surely one of them. Neither on a Lufthansa or Swiss Air or Air France flight could it happen – it is not even conceivable — that you would find on the lunch tray a folded slip of paper, with two prayers for grace formed with words taken from psalms: "For those who wish to join with us in saying grace."

In a still slightly aggressive mood, for better or for worse I went about inspecting what was worth seeing in the airport. I began by looking more closely at the larger than life-sized bronze figure in the entrance hall. It was the figure of a man wearing a cowboy hat. On the plinth was the brief inscription: "Texas Ranger 1960. One riot, one Ranger." It was also noted that the statue was a gift from "Mr. and Mrs. Wyatt." By chance, a giant Texan was sauntering by. He, too, was wearing the broad-brimmed hat, and he resembled the statue also in other ways. I asked him to explain about the "Texas Ranger." With a certain air of complacency he told me about a riot which this powerful policeman had single-handedly "sorted out" just by appearing on the scene. When I commented that in the meantime there were some riots — for example, at universities — which could not be "sorted out" by *one* Ranger, the Texan shrugged his shoulders and went on his way without another word.

In the window of a souvenir shop several right-angled boards were mounted like paintings to be marveled at. The boards were rough-hewn and loosely put together. On them, in lines one above the other like notes of music, were three or four pieces of barbed wire about thirty or forty centimeters long, each piece shaped differently. Beside each line was the name of the inventor and a date. A person appeared beside me unnoticed, who, as I then saw, had with a smile detected my surprise. "You are wondering about the meaning of these pieces of wire?" "Yes! Surely there were no concentration camps in Texas." "No, naturally not." These were, instead, the different sorts of barbed wire used in earlier times to fence in the cattle. But then this friendly man, who had already walked on, came back again and whispered to me: "But yes, we did have concentration camps here: for the Japanese from California after the attack on Pearl Harbor."

The bookshop had a special surprise waiting for me. Without going in, I looked at the paintings and books on display outside. As was to be expected, seven years after the murder of John F. Kennedy there were a dozen different representations on sale – in black and white or in color – of that macabre scenario, with an exact indication of where the President's car was and also of the window from which, as we now know, the lethal shot was *not* fired. What really happened has not been cleared up even to this day, since it has not been possible to identify the real assailants, let alone bring them before the courts. And it makes you wonder that the version which has been proven false is still be marketed in thousands of copies. — But no, something else seemed to me really surprising: the largest and most strikingly displayed shelf of best-sellers, i.e., the books which in this strange city were most likely to appeal to readers, were the Heidi stories by Johanna Spyri! Heidi in Dallas — who could have invented that?

But a few minutes before my next flight I was to experience something unexpected, something I did not at first understand. Instead of the usual free choice of a seat, passengers were scrutinized for a moment by a smart woman and were then given a number which was stuck to the boarding card. The meaning of this whole procedure only became clear when you looked around the interior of the airplane. Clear: the black people sat together in a group, which was only right.

When I arrived in Santa Fe someone immediately whispered to me that this was a very critical and unfavorable time. Another person who heard him contradicted and said, also in a whisper, that, on the contrary, this was exactly the right moment. With Jacqueline Denissoff and her husband I had driven immediately to Santa Fe; at the sumptuous meal to greet us, naturally the Bloody Mary featured. Then they had brought me a long way out of the city to the former seminary. The "staff," the organizers of the course on which I was collaborating, had gathered for a meeting which featured on the program as a sort of post-mortem. It was "half-time" in the first course, which, like the one which immediately followed, was of a month's duration. It was planned that I would participate in the second half of the first course and in the first half of the second. When Jacqueline and I arrived they were just on the point of arranging a discussion group. Jacqueline's husband had preferred to wait for her outside in the car. I introduced my companion as the goddaughter of Jacques Maritain, which elicited surprise and lively interest, especially since Jacqueline in no way concealed her French/Russian charm. She took her leave soon after, and the faces became serious again. The post-mortem began. I wanted to attend it and look for my room afterwards. I could not wish for a better opportunity to get to know the staff and the situation. A Dutch Jesuit, quite informally and without invitation, took the floor and with unusual severity attacked the initiator of the course and its overall concept. Under attack was the Dominican Blasé Schauer; he was a student chaplain and had become convinced that modern Christianity had to regain "the art of celebrating" — by which he meant, more precisely, giving renewed life to the sacred signs and symbols in the sacramental sphere and in the liturgy as a whole. A year earlier he had visited me in Münster, and I had immediately found his plan convincing. The Dutch Jesuit, a high-spirited man, clearly did not find it easy to moderate his choice of words; he called the whole thing reactionary, pre-conciliar and Thomistic. I knew that my book about feasts, which had been translated into English, had been especially recommended to participants in the course, and so I felt that the word "Thomistic" was meant as a criticism aimed at me. Some members of the group looked over at me expectantly. But the Reverend Schauer, who was not going to let go of the reins so easily, did not lose his composure; he had presumably experienced this argumentative theologian before. So, instead of answering, he took the floor to make a short speech of welcome, in which he introduced me to the circle. Then, without any formal ritual, he told me the names and functions of some members of the staff. The most prominent guest was the Director of the French National Council for the Liturgy, P. Pierre-Marie Gy, who was also a Dominican, a quiet man ready for compromise but also quite critical. As I later found out, he was well known to my friends Pasher and Volk. And he did not accept without reserve the impulsive behavior of his young religious comrade. Then there was the young

red-haired American Jesuit, James Dockery, who had done his doctorate at Berkeley University in the department of Speech and
Drama. We soon struck up a friendly relationship and enjoyed a
lot of laughs. Also present, though not taking any direct part in
the course, was the architect John McHugh, who lived nearby. He
had built the famous, ingeniously conceived Santa Fe Opera in the
desert of New Mexico and also revamped the uninspired interior
of the seminary church, a little in the style of Ronchamp. The
Dutch Jesuit, who was meant to be responsible for "modern church
music," was quite ostentatiously passed over. But he had already
announced that he would soon be leaving. Two women, the only
ones in the group, were the last to be named. One of them, sitting
near me, had — by the impatient jigging up and down of her
dancer's foot in its elegant shoe — already sufficiently attracted
my attention and made me curious. She was Vera Sorina, who had
in fact years ago trained with the Bolshoi Ballet and was now active
as an actress and director; she was still, vibrating like a race-horse,
full of aggressive and vital intelligence. Now, in collaboration with
James Dockery, she had a particularly important role to play in the
program of the course. She was, by the way, married to one of the
wealthiest managers of a big American radio company and she was,
besides — something I heard only after my departure — an Oblate
of the Benedictine Order. The other woman belonging to the staff
was a Dominican nun, distinguishable by the slightly modernized
habit of her Order; earlier, although she was still quite young, she
had been director of an art school in Florence; she was now responsible for the artistic shaping of religious symbols and signs.

Vera Sorina suggested with obvious impatience that I respond
to the Dutchman's attack. But I wanted to keep my powder dry
and settled for a somewhat generally stated agreement with Pater
Schauer's conception. She was not satisfied with that, and she
made no secret of the fact. In the following weeks we did some
friendly verbal foil-fencing. As we parted company she asked me

for some of my books in the original German, and I received from her the splendid recording of Claudel's *Joan of Arc at the Stake* set to music by Honegger. It was the French version, in which she speaks superbly the role of Joan.

After the session on the first evening, which, because the post-mortem was focused on some technical deficiencies, left me none the wiser, I was led to an excellently appointed apartment which was to be mine for four weeks; it was probably, I thought, formerly the "Bishop's Room" in this seminary which was now spookily empty. The Bishop had moved his seat to Albuquerque. It seemed odd that the Dean and the Chaplain had remained in Santa Fe. Sometimes I saw a middle-aged man walking through the empty corridors. He would greet me silently. He wore an Indian head-band around his finely shaped intellectual's head. It was said that he had been a good chaplain.

On the following day there was an American-style breakfast with too much noise and hubbub: on the tables were packets of cornflakes, bags of cakes, cartons of milk; people took whatever tea, coffee, or fruit juice they wanted. It was all very loud, but cheerful. Afterwards, outside in the glorious fresh morning air, which was both light and warm, we held devotions consisting of a psalm, a reading and a hymn. I am constantly amazed at how quickly these Americans can switch from some ordinary everyday chat or a well-told joke to a real, spontaneously formulated prayer.

Around nine o'clock there was a lecture followed by discussion. Already on the first day it was my turn to speak on the theme: "What does 'sacred' mean?" For a change, as people immediately noted, the Dutch Jesuit participated in the discussion. I had hardly finished when he opened the discussion; and naturally he championed, in a very polemical tone, the fashionable cause of desacralization. There was then a heated debate in which he talked on so emotionally and unclearly that it was not difficult for me eliminate him from the contest and to win not only the audience's agreement but also their laughter. — Of course, there were also serious objections, especially to my later lectures ("What is a priest?", "What is a Church?"). But this man had already, once and for all, deprived Dutch Catholicism of all credit. And he was also prematurely true to his announcement: he left on the same day without a farewell.

For the midday meal we went up to the cafeteria of a liberal arts college, fifteen minutes away. Its president was a laicized Catholic auxiliary bishop, who in the meantime had married. And so we found ourselves in what was in many ways a "post-conciliar" situation. Walking to and from meals was particularly interesting for me because of the opportunities offered to have relaxed personal conversations with priests from all over the country — from San Francisco, the Midwest, and New York. And, in fact, as we sauntered along I heard some scarcely believable "true stories" which I thought even here — or precisely here — would have been impossible and which I must relate.

But first some particular aspects of our course need to be reported. The Mass celebrated daily in the late afternoon attracted quite a few people out from the city of Santa Fe. They were interested in the constantly changing symbols decorating the interior of the church and the images and photos sometimes projected onto the walls during Mass. The fact that the whole ceremony of the Mass, the sermon and the readings were discreetly video-recorded went completely unnoticed. But this was a particularly important point. This immediately reproducible documentation was played back to each of the celebrants and was critically analyzed with regard to gesture, tone of speech and vocabulary, in the context of an extremely discreet discussion to which no one except Vera Sorina and the Jesuit James Dockery was admitted. On the same evening a meeting of all participants had preceded this, in which all were invited individually to give their critical response. And there was plenty of cause for criticism. For instance, a priest from New York, a native of Italy, began his sermon by introducing himself as Christopher Ruggiero and adding the words: "Just call me Chris." Distributing the Eucharist he approached me with a smile and said: "Doctor Pieper, this is the body of Christ." It was somewhat difficult to make it clear to this nice cleric that, dressed as he was — as the *Missale Romanum* says — in "sacred" liturgical vestments – he was acting *in persona Christi*, for which reason his own name, and indeed the abbreviation of it reserved for his circle of friends, was just as much out of place as was the use of my name and my doctor title at the distribution of the Eucharist. He accepted with good grace my demand that, for the future, he avoid giving me his smile of complicity. – Shortly afterwards I remembered that my colleague Denissoff, Jacqueline's father, who many years ago had been kneeling beside me at the communion rails in an Eastern Rite College, had been asked my Christian name. But I was not addressed by this name; as I found out much later, the formula used was – unexpectedly objective and without any hint of private familiarity – simply: "The servant Josef partakes of the Body and Blood of Jesus Christ."

Never had I experienced an Indian fiesta, although this was now my fourth time in New Mexico. But now some of the sacred festivals celebrated with great solemnity in the villages around Santa Fe coincided in time with our course. And it was explicitly part of our program to visit the nearby Indian settlements on their main festival days: Santa Anna, Santo Domingo and another community bearing a somewhat splendid English name, the patron saint of which was the Apostle James (Santiago). The festival started on this very Feast of St. James in Park View. The parish was run by Franciscans, and crowds of mostly young monks in the brown habits of the Brothers Minor streamed in to celebrate the Feast Day. The colorful procession which followed the solemnly celebrated High Mass was joined by a humble, small group of Indians, who at the end, without attracting much attention, performed their dances; but it was fundamentally a festival reminiscent of Santiago de Compostela or even Seville, although the Spanish still spoken exclusively at Mass was suddenly extinguished by the English language, like the words featuring on the exterior wall of the church exhorting us to "Smile! God loves you!" — something that would be inconceivable anywhere else in the world outside America.

Still, there was, in the procession, the beautiful sight of a long line of young women wearing white lace veils over a perpendicularly placed comb in their black hair. Above all, there was the troop of Caballeros de Santiago in magnificent garb, which galloped ahead of the procession and then charged back to join it. They also bore the flags and banners which exactly described the program of festivities: after the American and then the Papal flag came the flag of the old fleet of the Spanish Empire ("red and gold, with the lion of Léon and the tower of Castile"); and even the emblems of the Habsburgs and the Bourbons were not missing.

At the end of the procession under the July sun, the Franciscans invited us to an improvised but quite sumptuous meal in the parish house. The monks had in the meantime taken off their habits and now looked more like young cowboys. In the animated conversation it was soon revealed that I was the author of some books which quite a few of them had had to read for their examinations, and so my chair in the shade was surrounded by a small group of willing servants who plied me with special delicacies and with almost too much whisky.

Ten days later, a completely different scenario: a completely Indian Fiesta in Santo Domingo! — I stayed during this excursion as close as possible to an unusually well-informed Señor Suarez who had been prepared to accompany us. He had Indian blood himself. His grandmother, who was from Santo Domingo, was expelled from the tribe when a Spanish-speaking American, a "Chicano," married her. But her grandson had many friends amongst the Indians in this same settlement. And naturally he had very detailed knowledge of the rituals involved in the Fiesta about to be celebrated.

On this day, hundreds of enthusiastic sight-seeing Americans came from far away to Santo Domingo. They were immediately led by quite business-like Indians to well-built parking lots and were thus kept a due distance away from their village. Together with the ticket for parking — which cost a good five dollars — they were handed a notice on which were listed a whole series of prohibitions which Americans found seriously constricting, and the observance of which would be strictly enforced, as would be seen later: "absolutely" no photography, no tape-recording, and no alcohol!

When we arrived, the festival was already in full swing. Up to two hundred men and women, separated by sex into rows of four, formed a closed block of dancers who hardly moved from the spot. All the women had bare feet, so that, as our companion said, the fruitfulness of the earth could come up into their wombs; all the men wore boots, but they were naked above the waist. In the direct sunshine you could see the sweat streaming down their chests. The dance consisted of a rocking movement of the body and a rhythmic stamping of the feet. The women held pine branches in their hands and the men had pumpkin rattles full of seeds. A choir of thirty to forty men, likewise not changing its position, sang an accompaniment. The words of their song, consisting of purely vocalized calls, are fixed and unchangeable; and, as we were told, the dancers were not permitted any deviation from the rhythm – the details of which we were not able to grasp. After the dance had lasted several hours with short breaks, the dancers, who must have been completely exhausted, went off in single file to an enclosure made of green branches; it was erected in the middle of the square, in which stood the statue of the Holy One; before they entered, they were handed bread and candles by old women, which they then laid before the Holy One and then later gave them, as now consecrated gifts, to be distributed amongst the villagers. Finally, the men go down into the underground place of worship (Kiwa) which no one else was allowed to enter. Only the top steps of a ladder were visible at the entrance. Down there they divested themselves of the ritual garments they had been wearing. The tourists clapped in prolonged applause, as if the whole thing had been a play or a folklore presentation. But the Indians — and this, too, can be seen on the notice — consider the dance a prayer which says to "God, our Father, that we love him – as Dominic also did, in his own way." We heard from our companion that it was unthinkable for him, say during a dance, to greet his friends and to chat with them about this and that; they would all even behave as if they did not know one another. "As long as they are wearing their sacred garb they are in another world."

On the same evening, during the critical discussion of the celebration of Mass, with a certain cunning I introduced this very point with the forthright statement that this matter, which the Indians take for granted, was highly relevant for us "post-conciliar" Christians. I have sometimes seen a priest, still in his vestments after celebrating Mass, going to the area outside the church door to chat with his parishioners and even smoke a cigarette. My thesis was that here was an instance of relinquishing one of the *praeambula sacramenti*. Again, it was not at all easy to explain to these clerics the meaning of the "sacred vestments" and to convince them that the priest who celebrates this "sacred act" is really, for this length of time, in an "other" world. — We had, indeed, extraordinarily much to learn from the Indians about the "art of celebrating."

I was not able to find what sort of relationship, on the whole, these Indians had with the Church. Their forefathers had been converted to Christianity by the Franciscans more than three hundred years ago. No satisfactory answers were forthcoming. Twenty years earlier (1950) one of the missionaries in Santa Fe told me that, from time to time, a girl would be sent to him with the message that it would be better if he stayed away from the community the following Sunday. Someone said: "On that day they would be doing their heathen dream dances." I had already heard the rites commemorating the dead in the "Kiwa." The "worship of ancestors" was mentioned. This elicited my question: what was understood by the word "heathen"? The unambiguous answer I received was: "Honoring of false gods!" — One of our course participants, a parish priest in Albuquerque, said that, to his knowledge no Indian – at least, no one from the Pueblos tribe — had ever become a priest; and when in 1954 or 1955 three young Indians entered the seminary their people simply killed them. I could hardly believe it. What a country!

But on our way to the midday meal I heard a completely incredible "Indian story" which I would not have accepted as true had it not been told by the person whom it directly concerned. Place of the action: Isleta, an Indian village in New Mexico. Main actor: the parish priest of the community, a native of Germany. The Indians in Isleta had the custom, on the day after Christmas, of bringing the crib out of the church, putting it in a hut made of foliage which they had erected in the square, and then dancing before the Christ Child. The priest found this an un-Christian custom and decided to put an end to it. He knew, of course, that the Indians could only dance on the naked earth, so the idea occurred to him to lay concrete over the whole square – which then happened. But the Indians enjoy a certain autonomy regarding jurisdiction and policing. They summoned the priest to appear before their council, and there they asked him solemnly if he intended to abolish the religious practices of their tribe. The priest, obviously an intrepid type, declared that dancing in front of the Christ Child was an un-Christian custom that he would not tolerate. They then handcuffed him and brought him to the edge of the reservation where he was released and it was made clear to him that he was not to show his face there again. At this point in the story I stopped. Then I asked: "How long ago was that?" — "Exactly five years." — "So, it happened in 1965?" — "Yes! But what is coming now is the really 'medieval' part." Now the Bishop stepped in. He could not simply pass over what had happened; he had to do something. But what he then did was awful: he imposed an interdict, i.e., he forbad all divine service in the community apart from Extreme Unction. This caused suffering amongst the Indians, but they did not yield. And the Bishop, too, stayed with his decision. "So the tragedy has already gone on for five years. What happens now?" I gathered from the tone of the narration that the story must have had a happy ending. "The Bishop raised the interdict and appointed another parish priest for Isleta: namely me! Next month I take over my new office." "And what will you do?" — "My first directive has already been carried out: the square has been cleared of concrete!"

Strangely, the participants in the second course which, in the meantime had begun, were of a quite different kind from those of the first. — During the midday walk to the cafeteria I noticed a young priest whom I had seen running around in blue jeans in the morning but who, to my surprise, was now wearing the white Dominican habit. I greeted him with joy that was clear to see, and I did not hide my astonishment. And then I got to hear another "true story" — not an entirely incredible one, but one which I absolutely have to pass on. Curiously, he began by explaining that he always wanted to wear the habit only after midday. And also his "story" had to do with this white habit of the Order of Preachers.

He said he wore it on the street in San Francisco; in saying this he seemed to be challenging me — as if he was waiting for a reaction; and indeed I was truly surprised, and I said it to him. But what he then said was even more amazing. This open showing of his belonging to a religious order was, he was convinced, one of the reasons why the small Californian Dominican Province, which had less than two hundred monks, had twice as many novices as the two other much bigger provinces – with over a thousand members — put together. And then he began, warming to his task, to give details. In Oakland, the centre of his province, the monks — mainly the younger ones — resisted the suggestion of their brethren that they should leave off the religious habit and instead of living in the monastery take an apartment in the city. Precisely this successful protest — keeping the habit and continuing to live in the monastery — had been the reason that so many young men flocked to them as novices. Such processes deserve to be recorded and made known.

There was also an addendum to this story, and it was again about the priest's religious habit. I asked my companion about his work and about any plans he had, and he answered that something new had cropped up for him. Recently he had been invited to take on the role of counselor and also a kind of psychotherapist in a big, explicitly non-Christian clinic which was funded by private donations and had a purely humanitarian orientation. "And when I presented myself, just a few weeks ago, in civilian dress — which was unusual for me, but which seemed appropriate for the occasion — the doctor in charge shook his head vigorously when he saw me. 'No, no, that's exactly what we don't want!' You have to be identifiable as a priest. That's what this is about.'"

On our way back from the cafeteria, Vera Sorina hurried to catch up with me and called back over her shoulder, although she was herself engaged in lively conversation: "Marvelous that a fresh breeze is blowing into Carmel!" A few days previously, after a thundery shower, I had strolled down the Mount Carmel Road in the gloriously fresh evening, and, looking over the garden fence of the convent, had observed a nun who was digging the soil with a spade. "Is that the right work for a nun?" We had a brief conversation. She was the "Extern Sister" who was the only one permitted to leave the cloister to run the necessary errands. My name was not unknown to her and she regretted that the Carmelite sisters could not hear my lectures in the auditorium across the road; to this end they would love to "remove the windows." I then suddenly suggested that I come into the convent and speak to the sisters there if they would like me to. At first, she could not believe it and said she was "overjoyed." The following morning I made my first visit to a convent of such strict observance. In the anteroom I was standing not in front of a door but a revolving panel, behind which I could hear a nun who remained invisible. I gave my name and was asked to go into the reception room. One of the walls consisted of a perpendicular latticework trellis. The curtain behind it was drawn a few minutes later, and before me stood the Prioress, charmingly natural — a blooming young woman, who welcomed me as a guest in the house. We immediately discussed the possible and desirable themes; and again there was cause for amazement: precisely the most difficult ones were chosen. Already on the next day I was to begin with the theme: "What is the meaning of 'God speaks'?" – At the midday meal I watched out for Vera Sorina to say to her: if we are talking about a fresh breeze, it seems to be blowing from the convent to me rather than the reverse.

Scene changes happen in this country sometimes so suddenly and so radically that, even when a person anticipates a change there is always an element of surprise. This happened to me when the young Prior of the Benedictine Monastery of Pecos urged me to accompany him to a prayer meeting of the "Pentecostal movement." The surprise began while we were on our way. We wanted to break the journey to the monastery with a quick evening snack. I had been a guest there three or four times since 1950, the last occasion being two years previously. But the atmosphere of the house had changed in a way that was incomprehensible to me. When we arrived, the meal in the "refectory" — which was no longer referred to as such — had already begun. The Prior's place — which he thought was not worthy of mention — had been occupied by a middle-aged woman; she was, as I discovered, a nun. Everyone was sitting in a colorful circle around the table, chatting cheerily, while rather cheap popular music resounded from the ceiling. Someone asked where these "wonderful" tunes were coming from. The Prior casually answered that a two-hour tape was playing. Not the slightest suggestion of the requirement in the *Regula* of St. Benedict that the monks observe deep silence during the reading at table. Again and again someone would stand up and take from a sideboard the drink he wanted — milk, fruit juice, Coca Cola. A neighbor, thinking that that's what a German would want, put a can of Budweiser beer in front of me. He was wearing a bright-red pullover, and I heard with astonishment that he was a Trappist. There were certainly quite a few priests and religious in the group, but it was not possible to tell from their clothing. Afterwards I could understand that, as we met to start off on the journey, the Prior was not joking — as I had thought at first — when he had said I should leave off the tie which I had put on to be on the safe side. "Take that off, we are quite informal." The Trappist was also traveling with the Prior and me to the prayer meeting of the "Pentecostals." We were soon on our way there.

In the spacious living room of an obviously well-to-do middle-class man in this small town, up to twenty-five people had already gathered — young and old, but clearly fewer men than women. The rows of chairs formed an oval shape. I was keen to find a place on the outer circle and to remain as hidden as possible. The meeting had not yet begun; we were welcomed by the person presiding — seemingly the woman of the house. They had probably been awaiting the arrival of the Prior, whom everyone seemed to know; but during the meeting he abstained from saying anything. He did sing along lustily during the first song, which was accompanied by a guitarist and, through the use of microphones and loudspeaker, was raised to an almost unbearable pitch. The "text" consisted of the single word "Amen" which was endlessly repeated and accompanied by rhythmical hand-clapping. The group, by now almost a congregation, already felt that they had now been "prepared." At the invitation of the leader to anyone who wanted to "give witness" there began a long series of personal, sometimes very private, sometimes very trivial testimonies about prayers being answered, divine protection, "influence of the Spirit" — at which the constant answer in unison was "Praise the Lord!" Then another song, which this time begins with the words "I get so thrilled with Jesus." Finally, after the session had lasted two to three hours and by which time the air had become stifling, a row of chairs was placed in the empty space in the middle of the oval, and anyone who wanted to say a special prayer or felt they wanted the congregation to pray over them or to pray for "spiritual baptism" for them was requested to take a seat there. After some hesitation the seats were occupied. Their concerns were named without reserve, and sometimes without the slightest hint of discretion: one person is faced with a difficult decision; one woman, probably known to many of the participants, wants "to become a better mother and wife" — and so on. At that point others approach the supplicants, stand behind them or kneel beside them on the floor and "lay hands on them," meanwhile touching them on head or shoulders or thighs — while in the whole room a prayer begins with wordless humming. On the faces – of the women, above all – signs of hypnotic ecstasy become visible. In any case, I say to myself, here there are several things at work which have nothing to do with prayer or any kind of religious acts. And all my instincts, particularly the Catholic ones, react with a clear and decisive "no!"

During the long return journey to Santa Fe at night I did hardly anything but argue with the Prior, who, unbelievably, seemed quite taken with it all, whereas I could not comprehend that a Benedictine was at all able to engage with something which was, strictly speaking, nothing but crazy fantasy, as if the working of the Holy Spirit could not only be defined in time and space but could also be conjured up.

The next day in Santa Fe I described my experience and did not conceal my concerns. An elderly priest, a monsignor, whom I had not yet seen in our group, invited me to accompany him to a prayer-meeting which was taking place in the Catholic University of Albuquerque and which would be of a much higher level than the one I had described. The monsignor looked like a solid, steady country Dean, and I accepted. But what I experienced there was even worse than the living-room meeting.

But first I have to describe another "scene change," which took me, like Habakkuk, by the hair of the head and placed me in the terrifying center of contemporary world history. As soon as you enter the unique home of the Santa Fe Opera, you come into a magically transformed world. It is built in the form of two oyster shells standing upright, with their hollow spaces facing one another but without touching at any point. You have the impression of being not inside but outside in the dry, warm mountain air of the desert of New Mexico. The atmosphere is, in fact, so light and thin that, as I was told, dance on the stage becomes impossible and has to be cut — even the ballet that this evening was meant to be performed for the early Stravinsky opera about the Chinese nightingale. On this occasion there is no back to the stage; instead, the audience sees, on this 6th of August 1970, a slightly clouded firmament above the dark landscape, against which the new crescent moon shone brightly. Taking a deep breath I felt transported out of the real world – until the moment when my neighbor leaned over to me and, pointing just past the side of the stage, whispered: "That is Los Alamos, where the atom bomb was conceived; twenty-five years ago today it destroyed Hiroshima."

And so a few days later I drove in my country Dean's car to Albuquerque. About eighty people, among them a number of students of either sex, were gathered in the diner. The sight of the microphones all around us was no good sign; and, in fact, the music band began a song at a sign from its leader — a lay theologian and university lecturer. The song was now sung, all four verses, at full volume. The monsignor, who had taken a seat with me on the outer part of the circle, joined in vigorously with the general rhythmical hand-clapping. But Père Gy, who to my surprise I discovered was sitting opposite me, likewise in the outer circle of chairs, clapped no more than I did. Some stood while they were singing, with their arms raised ecstatically and with rapt expressions. A student, in the embrace of a young man, beat the rhythm with an Indian pumpkin rattle and seemed from the very beginning to be transported out of this world. In fact, the manic expression on the face of many women suggested they were out of themselves. It was a new experience for me that in pauses between songs, along with the personal statements "giving witness" there were exhortations, in the name of God, directed at all of us — sometimes by young girls hardly twenty years old; with their eyes closed, they began their message mostly with the words "My Children …" The gathering listened in silence and then answered with a loud "Praise the Lord!" It was an absolute surprise when a man then spoke "in tongues" for several minutes. Twenty years previously I had experienced this during a Revivalist meeting of black people in South Bend: beside me a black woman jumped up and in a loud voice emitted a string of meaningless words, which on this occasion did not surprise me. But now a robust man in his fifties, who could easily have been the owner of a garage, suddenly began to speak "in tongues"; he was sitting in the inner circle, directly opposite me, so that I could look directly at his face. I thought I could see by looking at him how difficult it must be — purely technically — to speak real words, i.e., sounds made up of consonants and vowels, which had no intelligible meaning. While I was not prepared to join in the loudly proclaimed "Praise the

Lord" after the brief silence that followed, I did feel a sense of amazement.

The leader of proceedings did not seem satisfied with the way things had gone; clearly, he said, there is someone in the room who is hindering the work of the Holy Spirit. I felt that I was the person in question. It had probably not escaped them that during a song everyone had sung, I had not, despite the explicit request, laid my hands on the shoulders of my neighbors and, as in the Rhine carnivals, swayed with the music. Now there were to be fervent prayers for this recalcitrant person. This happened in a song which was to be sung with arms raised. The title of the song was "Surrender." Since I did not, for my part, feel like raising my arms, the leader announced a break. The new arrivals were requested to go to the office for information, while the others were invited to refreshments ("fellowship with coffee or iced tea").

The Dean agreed on an early departure for Santa Fe. With his very fast car he could easily have run over some Indians who had probably drunk too much firewater and were strolling at a leisurely pace along the highway. Not a word was spoken about the meeting. My disappointment was clear enough. I was surprised and not a little unsettled to hear that the Monsignor was in some way or other assigned to the convent of the Carmelite nuns.

I went to the nuns in the convent at least a dozen times. Behind the trellis, not only did they listen with a level of attention that I found stimulating, but they engaged in a highly intelligent and amazingly animated discussion. When the inevitable question arose about a suitable honorarium for me, I asked that the convent arrange for a memorial Mass to be celebrated for my son Thomas — which then took place before my departure. After the Mass, without my requesting it, the *Adore te* was sung — not in Latin, but, as I was told later, in the splendid English translation by Gerard Manley Hopkins.

Ever since, at Christmas each year a friendly letter arrives from the Prioress in Santa Fe. Last year (1984) a second letter was added in which the youngest sister of the convent, whom I had not as yet known, introduced herself in her clear and intelligent handwriting as a reader of my books. She had become not only a Catholic but also a Carmelite, and now, for the rest of her life would pray for me. Naturally, an author does not mind hearing that kind of thing. But what gives me joy and consolation is the fact that this young American, without realizing it, was following in the footsteps of Sister Rotrudis, the Icelandic-Westphalian nun.

VI

Rome and Krakow

In Easter Week 1974, after a cool morning walk in Rome I entered
the Secretariat of the International Thomas Congress, which was
to be held in memory of my great teacher. At that moment I did
not realize in what a surprising way the two names, Rome and
Krakow, would become linked together in my memory. From the
Caetani Palace, in which Hubert Howard had yet again kindly reserved the guest room for me, it was only a few minutes' walk to
the "Angelicum," which is now called "Università San Tommaso
d'Aquino." As I went in the door a German colleague greeted me
and commented in amusement, but as a warning, that the organization of the Congress was rather "Italian" in style. I soon had a
sense of this myself. As programs were being handed out and I
asked for some sort of receipt for the pre-payment in dollars I had
sent, giving me the right to receive the Proceedings of the Congress, the reply came promptly: "That is no problem." Then I was
handed a piece of paper quickly torn from a page that was already
written on. An illegible signature was scribbled on the scrap of
paper, which was hardly the size of a postage stamp. As I was passing one of the information stands and putting the ludicrous "receipt" in my wallet, an American student sprang out and shook my
hand enthusiastically. He was from Massachusetts and knew me
from somewhere. After a short conversation, rather emphatically
he gave me some advice in parting: "If there is any way I can help
you, please look me up." Somewhat puzzled, I thanked him and

went on my way to the conference room. It was, unexpectedly, a gigantic Auditorium Maximum which seemed fitted out with a multiple translation system for the congress of more than a thousand "Thomists" from all parts of the world. The first *sessio plenaria* was already in progress; unfortunately, the lecture by Fernand von Steenberghen had just finished. When I tried to apologize to him, he shook his head and took me aside, and we recalled the rather adventurous journey we had shared from Indiana to Ohio in 1950 in the car of our friend Denisoff. Again it became apparent to me that such unplanned conversations and encounters were particularly enjoyable and were perhaps the best part of a congress.

Like this I also met, in a small group during the midday break, the Dominican James A. Weisheipl from the Canadian Institute of Medieval Studies. He had just published his excellent book — which I saw only later — on *The Friar Thomas d'Aquino*. I would never have thought that, after the vast flood of specialist writings, anything could still be written by a single author. The Canadian was amused to hear me explain the original meaning of his Bavarian surname. Naturally, he had not known it. And during the meal, while the waiter spontaneously kept on putting new carafes of red wine on the table, there was a great deal of hearty laughter.

But by far the most important meeting was to come only on the following day. I would give a lot today if I could say how it came about and what the first words were which I exchanged with Cardinal Karol Wojtyla. Undoubtedly, he was the only prelate of this rank who was competent to take an active part in the discussions. We had an immediate understanding; and the former Philosophy Professor from Lublin seemed to know about me. In any case, it was both welcome and unexpected to hear from him — something he repeated several times the following day: "You absolutely must come to Poland!"

There was a surprise on the third day of the congress: meeting Yves Congar again. He was to speak in the same plenary session as I was. He was speaking about the Holy Spirit in the Ethics of Thomas Aquinas, and I about Elements of the Concept of "Creaturehood." During the *Semaine des Intellectuels* in Paris in 1951, together with Gabriel Marcel and Jean Daniélou we had held lectures on the same theme in an evening session, and had not seen one another since. But I was surprised and shocked when I now saw him in his white Dominican habit laboriously making his way into the auditorium on crutches. Anticipating my question, he said with a dismissive gesture that it was "something or other neurological." Of course, when he was sitting beside me and spoke from the podium with almost youthful energy and incisive vehemence, no one was thinking of this wretched "neurological" thing — least of all himself. In retrospect, I was annoyed that I held my lecture in English, as did, later, Cardinal Wojtyla. Karl Rahner was the only one who had announced that his lecture would be in German. But people were surprised and disconcerted to find at short notice that this was not acceptable.

Although in the printed program there was no mention of the fact that Paul VI would visit the congress, it had been widely talked about in Rome. And it was this visit that reminded me of my American student's advice which I had not taken altogether seriously, and luckily I ran into him at the right moment. Although I arrived early, I found the auditorium already full, apart from the front rows, and clearly many people who had nothing to do with the congress were there for no other reason than to see the Pope. The organizers had either neglected or forgotten to watch the side door entrances to the room. The young man from Massachusetts, happy to see me again, congratulated me and led me immediately to a seat reserved for guests of honor. What I then, after a while, was able to observe from almost too close proximity turned out to be for me a depressing experience. You could only look with deep sympathy on this obviously sick old man, suffering under the burden of his office. His face, which looked sad and had in the

114

meantime become stiff, was exposed to public curiosity. With an fixed expression he listened patiently to the speech of welcome given by the host and organizer of the Congress, the General of the Dominican Order; then he made a speech himself without gesture or change of facial expression. On the whole, despite all the official rites for the occasion, or perhaps because of them, it was an almost painful sight.

Roccasecca Castle, where Thomas was born, the Fossanova monastery in which he died, the Abbey of Montecassino where he was sent to school as a boy — all of these places which I had not seen were, according to the plan, to be visited by the congress on its way from Rome to Naples, where it was then to be continued and concluded. But naturally, even if the organization had not been "Italian," it was an adventurous and risky undertaking to bring a congress with more than a thousand participants such a long way in buses to a different conference venue. But still I went with high expectations, which were naturally mixed with a degree of skepticism, to the Piazza Venezia, where it was comforting to see a long line of modern buses standing ready. But then my skepticism was seen to be warranted. Although I had taken the caution of arriving a good half hour before the arranged time of departure, it was only by sheer luck that I managed to get the last free seat. All the buses were completely full. The unlucky ones who, understandably, thought arriving a quarter of an hour early was sufficient, stood in disappointment on the footpath amongst an ever growing crowd of people. Clearly the exact number of passengers had not been established, and it was definitely greater than the number of participants in the Congress; in my bus, for instance, a young American lecturer, with his wife and three small children, took up four or five seats. Telephoning around Rome on that Sunday morning in search of still available buses eventually proved to be of no avail. Those waiting outside had to be advised, for better or for worse, to go directly to Naples — passing by the memorial sites. We did not yet know whether we, too, would miss seeing Roccasecca and Montecassino. At the very moment we were setting out, the Mass in Fossanova which we were meant to be celebrating together was due to begin; but for another reason, which also had not been anticipated, it had to be considerably delayed. Naturally, hundreds of us wanted to see and enter the room in the monastery where Thomas had died. It was situated on the top floor, and the stairway leading to it was so narrow that the people climbing the stairs could not pass those coming down. So it was well past midday when finally Cardinal Wojtyla, preceded by a long line of priests in alb and stole, arrived at the altar to celebrate Mass. If in his conversations with me I had admired his almost accent-free German I now had to admire even more the melodious sound of his Italian in his sermon about Thomas Aquinas. After Mass, we journeyed on to Aquino. There was nothing there to remind us of Thomas, but perhaps this little town had been chosen because of the possibility of a midday meal. But first, at the market-place, we had to endure the long speech of welcome delivered in Latin by the local Bishop, which was naturally directed mainly at the Cardinal. Then, to our horror, the mayor had to welcome us in his mother tongue. He, too, was not short of words. But then, when a brightly dressed crowd of flag-waving people entered the square, thinly disguised despair gripped the hungry participants of the Congress. After all, by now it was four o'clock in the afternoon. There seemed to be no end to the colorful display. My neighbor pointed out to me a cluster of people pushing and shoving around one of the bus organizers. It seemed that meal vouchers were being handed out, and in fact I was given a slip of paper on which the words "San Germano" were almost illegibly scribbled. We were told it was the name of a restaurant in the town. A small group of us were heading off to it when we were met by others who told us the shattering news that the "San Germano" was hopelessly overcrowded; but there was, a kilometer outside the town, a restaurant which had already been told about us and was prepared to serve us a dinner. We were soon sitting in a pleasant and spacious dining room. The round tables were laid for dinner, and in the middle of them were some bottles of red wine and baskets with white bread. Unfortunately, there was only one waiter and, each time he emerged from the kitchen, with drops of perspiration on his forehead and juggling some plates of food, he was greeted with loud applause. In the meantime, the diners, who had taken their place at table without any particular plan, started with the bread and wine, and, despite everything, the mood was good. Above all, there was the advantage of unplanned encounters. After we had all chatted for a while, it turned out that the man sitting next to me at table — who, from his language I suspected was a Jugoslav — was the Dominican Tomas Veres from Zagreb. Years ago I had sent him, at his request, a parcel of books by J. P. and in return I had asked that the monastery celebrate a memorial Mass for my son Thomas. Delighted by this chance meeting with someone he had known way back, he thanked me again in glowing terms and assured me that he and his brethren had, of course, immediately carried out my request.

When between midday and evening we returned to the town and to the waiting buses, it very soon became clear to us, without a word being spoken, that we would not see Roccasecca or Montecassino, although we had looked forward to them so much. We were only told that we were to board the bus which bore the name of the Neapolitan hotel assigned to us. For many, this involved changing buses as well as shifting luggage that had been stowed away and was not easy to find. During this bothersome procedure, at which the ill-tempered driver did not move a hand, I met Pater Norbert Luyten, the natural philosophy scholar from Freiburg in Switzerland. He would be staying, like myself, in the hotel "Presidente." We immediately became allies in expectation of the adventures that obviously lay ahead of us: the drivers were saying, even before we set off, that they were Romans and were not familiar with Naples, so that they would leave us at the main train station in Naples. When our painfully overcrowded bus arrived – the fourth or fifth to do so – it was already becoming dark, and at the Stazione Centrale in Naples there were no more taxis to be seen. When finally one did return, Pater Luyten, with amazing alacrity rushed up to it, tore the door open and threw his little bag into it. He had really "captured" the vessel! We breathed a sigh of relief. Success! But that was, unfortunately, an error — as we soon found out. At reception in the hotel thirty or forty participants were crowding around; there were indignant cries of protest ("No single rooms? Impossible!") Again I could only wonder at the initiative of the Padre, who succeeded — if only after a long wait — in securing for us two single rooms with a shared bathroom. We congratulated one another, but in the meantime we were so exhausted that we decided to go straight to bed without eating supper. In the spacious lift of the probably three-storied hotel we met Cardinal Wojtyla again. He seemed fresh, and not at all tired; in any case, he was studying the menu with interest. He smiled as he looked at us and said: "Chicken chasseur — that sounds good!"

It was an unhappy choice to move the Congress to Naples, if only because the sessions took place by turns at different venues. Besides, I was fed up with the learned discussions and preferred to saunter through the city, with which I was already somewhat familiar. In the monastery San Domenico Maggiore I visited Saint Thomas's cell and at the marketplace the grave of the young Konradin von Hohenstaufen. Unfortunately, I missed Cardinal Wojtyla's lecture. It was planned for 23 April, but I had promised my wife I would be home on that day, since it was our wedding anniversary. When I was leaving the breakfast room on my last morning I saw the Cardinal sitting with a group of his Polish friends. I took my leave of him and asked him how seriously he meant the repeated invitation to Poland. He said: "You will soon see how s eriously it is meant!" While I was on my way through the hall to the taxi which was already waiting outside, the coordinator of the Congress caught up with me, out of breath, and asked in English if I had already spoken with the "Registrar"; I was not aware that there was a Registrar, nor did I know his name, nor where I could have met him. "Well, you are a member of our 'Scientific Committee,' and besides, you gave a lecture; you will receive a honorarium of 100,000 Lire. We will send you a check." I knew that that sum would, at the most, cover half of my travel costs, and so I forgot about it for the time being. But then followed a little drama which was not without a touch of criminality. After a while, a letter arrived with the check enclosed, which went, as it usually would, directly to the postal-check office. But strangely I heard nothing for weeks. When I inquired, I was told that a foreign check was normally sent first to the Central Bank of the region; but it seemed that problems were found there. I innocently made inquiries at this public bank and found that they were engaged in finding out by what illegal means I had come to receive this check. The amount had been sent from a blocked account. My description of what had happened seemed to convince them, and soon the money appeared in my account.

And now the Thomas Congress was once and for all behind me, and I was beginning to wait for news from Poland. But summer and winter and again summer came; and only in the following winter did an invitation to Krakow arrive for February 1976.

Although the thought of Poland kept on coming to mind, these years were, of course, by no means idle. There was far too much to do. For three semesters I had weekly lectures and seminars in the university. I had festivities surrounding my seventieth birthday to contend with. The first volume of my autobiography, finished after repeated rewrites, had to be prepared for printing. My collaborative critical examination of the German translation of the *Ordo Missae* kept me on tenterhooks. My friend Hermann Volk was expecting a ceremonial address on the occasion of the thousand-year celebration of his episcopal church in Mainz. He found the theme I first proposed rather unsettling: "Body Memory." Almost every day I would take my wife in her wheel-chair around the neighboring streets. Twice more, each time in July, the Americans brought me over to the Escorial for a series of lectures. I returned from a lecture tour in Canada — and it has to be said, to my shame, with a touch of alcohol poisoning. The doctor immediately forbade the drinking of all spirits — whisky, gin, and unfortunately the essential ingredient for making a Bloody Mary: vodka; but fortunately not wine — after a period of abstinence.

On a February afternoon in 1976, in Cologne I boarded a rather uncomfortable airplane of the type "Tupolev"; after a flight of two and a half hours I landed in Warsaw, where I was surprised to see that evening darkness had set in.

My reception was also surprising. I was greeted by a charming student with a bouquet of flowers. The priest who was expecting me was a theologian and Professor of the State University of Warsaw and thought this was appropriate. We first took a tram and then walked for fifteen minutes. But before I entered the house in which I was to live for a few days I had already learned quite a lot about the distinctive atmosphere of this supposedly communist-totalitarian People's Republic of Poland. The slightly French style of the ceremonial greeting was just the beginning. Then I was told that my quarters were in one of two semi-detached houses, in which the dividing wall had — "really" without authorization — been broken through to allow for building a chapel in which, equally without authorization, every day Mass was celebrated, and on Sundays up to eight times to accommodate the numbers. Finally, when I arrived at the door of this remarkable semi-detached house, a dimly-lit housing estate was pointed out to me. I could see nothing of particular interest about it. But then my colleague told me with a grin, but without any comment, how, at the official inauguration a few weeks previously it had been discovered that instead of the twelve blocks of building there were really only eleven, and the building materials delivered for the twelfth block had vanished without trace.

On my host's bookshelves I found an amazing amount of literature from the "West," partly recently published, and in English, French, and German. In a friendly gesture they had placed next to one another on the writing table four or five of my own books in Polish translation. There was one which a Polish publisher had produced in exile in Paris. I immediately recalled that, when my Munich publisher had asked whether in Warsaw there would be interest in this book ("Death and Immortality") he received an answer that surprised us: the Paris edition might well have been published in Poland. In the Pax publishing firm, which had published the first edition of my "On Love," by then out of stock, I was given a reception at a small banquet and was told that they were prepared to have me brought by car from Warsaw to Lublin.

But beforehand I took a few thought-provoking walks through the city, sometimes accompanied by Poles, sometimes alone. I went to the cathedral, in the outer wall of which the treads of a German tank had been inserted, and to the site of the former ghetto. In the churches there were people praying at all times of the day; young men were kneeling on the stone floors; in the well-lit confessionals a priest in white vestments would be ready to administer the sacrament. Conversation with their German guest was, understandably, sometimes difficult. I was puzzled by one thing, since I was not very clear how things had gone there; in the last year of bombing in the war we had enough cares of our own. And so I heard from my companion for the first time, when we were on the banks of the Weichsel as the mighty stream roared past us, as he pointed across the river with his outstretched arm: "Over there, just a few hundred meters away, were the Russians in 1944. For two whole months they did not move from the spot, while our forces, counting on help from the Russians, rose up against the German occupying forces and finally had to capitulate." I likewise did not know that six months before the end of the war, on Hitler's orders, Warsaw had been systematically destroyed.

At the University of Lublin I had my first lectures to negotiate. The students listened carefully and were perhaps a little too well-behaved. The text had to be translated for them, paragraph by paragraph. In a lively discussion which took place in the evening around a table, only the professors took part and only German was spoken. At the festive farewell meal, the Rector stood up — although there were only four of us present — to make a short speech which he concluded with a sly question: a puzzle about the spherical oilcake which had just been put on the table as a dessert. He was sure that I would not solve it. And he was indeed right. How was I come up with the idea that it was not a plum jam filling but a center of sugared rose leaves?!

My constant companion on these walks through the city which, in my memory, always seemed to be in late evening darkness, was the then rather young Ethics professor Tadeusz Styczeń with whom it was possible to speak without reserve about even the most delicate questions. Before the last war, half of the population of Lublin was Jewish. Martin Buber's "Chassidische Geschichten" originated from here, he told me. The name of the death camp Maidanek was mentioned by chance. It was obviously assumed I would not want to visit it. When I repeated a question I had asked about whether the name Katyn was familiar to the average young Pole, the answer sounded angry: "Every Pole knows Katyn!"

Tadeusz Styczeń also brought me by car to Krakow, and naturally we spoke on the way about Cardinal Wojtyla, who had taught philosophy in Lublin. Styczeń seems to have been his assistant. He revered him as a fatherly friend. "I call him 'Uncle'." When we arrived in Krakow it turned out that the Cardinal would not be returning from a conference that night and would be expecting me for dinner the following day. But I had hardly a free minute.

Indeed, I was confronted with a well- thought-out program for the two days of my visit: walks through a part of the city — one of the richest and most beautiful I know — that had not been destroyed; an evening meeting with the directors of the Znac Publishing House; lectures for students; a visit to the Auschwitz concentration camp. But most of all I was looking forward to meeting the Cardinal again.

When I saw him as I was brought into the dining room of the Bishop's residence where he was in conversation with some guests, I thought I saw a surprising change in him; he seemed tired and ten years older than he was. He greeted me warmly with an embrace and the kiss of peace. In answer to my concerned question about his health, he told me that Paul VI had asked him to give the Exercises in the Vatican in Lent; and now, night after night, he was working at writing down twenty-two lectures which had to be handed in beforehand in Italian.

In the meantime they have been published as a book, appearing in German as "Zeichen des Widerspruchs" [Signs of Contradiction]. On the dust-cover the publisher had quoted Bishop Klaus Hemmerle: it was "moving" to read today "what a cardinal said at that time not only to Pope Paul VI but also to himself." That reads as if the Archbishop of Krakow had had no idea of what was to happen to him later. But there are some grounds for thinking that the reality was different. In any case, it has been said again and again with some credibility that the Archbishop Karol Wojtyla, probably in the years of Vatican II, had sought out the Capuchin Padre Pio whom he had known in his student days; and this gifted monk, with his stigmata and visionary powers, had looked at his visitor and said "You will become Pope" and "I see blood." I now tried to establish the truth of this story, which I had found out about only ten years after our first meeting in Rome. My first request for information was directed to my Lublin colleague Tadeusz Styczeń, but his answer, which I fully understood, was that he would never have dared to ask the Pope about these things, even though he had previously called him "Uncle." During a chance encounter with the Bishop of Essen a short time later, the Padre Pio story came up in conversation, and Bishop Hengsbach, who was also familiar with it, said spontaneously that he could tell me something interesting with regard to it. Immediately after the Conclave of August 1978 at which John Paul I was elected as successor to Pope Paul VI, Cardinal Wojtyla visited him in Essen on the way back to Poland and told him, more in vague hints and gestures than in clear words, how depressed he was going into the Conclave that was just coming to an end; but he said, almost exuberantly, how deeply relieved he was about the recently concluded Papal election. Clearly he thought that this time Padre Pio – though his name was not mentioned — had got it wrong. Shortly after this conversation with me, on a visit to Rome Bishop Hengsbach found out from the Bishop of Padua, and had him confirm it, that in a small gathering the Pope himself had told the story of that encounter with Padre Pio. This Capuchin Padre Pio — who died in 1968 — said, more than ten years before the event, that he would become Pope, but also that he would have much suffering. Probably Johannes Paul II had related the story before the assassination attempt and understandably interpreted the mention of blood purely symbolically.

In any case, it can hardly be said that the bleary-eyed Cardinal who greeted me in Krakow in February 1976 had, while he was writing down the Lenten talks for Paul VI, any inkling of what was in store for himself.

Then, a good two years later something completely unexpected happened: namely, the newly elected Pope John Paul I suddenly died a month after being enthroned as Pope, and Cardinal Wojtyla set out on the journey to Rome to a new Conclave, knowing full well that it was now his turn.

And, as everyone knows, on 16 October 1978 the Cardinals elected the first Polish Pope.

But we are anticipating. In the late winter of 1976 we were gathered in the Renaissance glory of the Archbishop's Palace for an unexpectedly simple midday meal — simple even by comparison with my previous Polish experiences. The conversation flowed comfortably; no speech was made. I exchanged cheerful memories with the Cardinal, who was sitting opposite me, about the Thomas Congress we attended two years previously. Next to me at the table sat the Dean of the seminary. He announced to me that he would accompany me in the afternoon to the Auschwitz concentration camp. At this point he knew no more than anyone else that a few years later he would succeed our host as Bishop of Krakow.

On the way to Auschwitz I learned things about Catholic Poland which would amaze visitors from the West: for example, that the seminaries were full and in some places there was even a *numerus clausus*. On the return journey we were less inclined to talk. The sight of the incinerators, the starvation huts, the wall of death, women's hair that could not be utilized – all of that renders you speechless, even, it seems, when you are not seeing it for the first time. After a short shock you realize as a German that the information displayed on the walls is written in Polish, French and English, but not in German and, of course, also not in Russian. Unforgettable for me was the gallows on which the Commandant of Auschwitz was hanged: before his eyes the place of his gruesome activities. With incredulous dismay I had shortly before read the autobiography this man had been compelled to write in prison: the son of a Catholic family, he had originally wanted to become a priest. He was always competent in good and evil, successful and obedient — he had always considered and "performed" his duties as director of the extermination camp as a duty required by his superiors and as a purely organizational task.

The next day I traveled by train to Breslau, passing the cities Beuthen, Oppeln and Brieg, all of which now naturally have Polish names. It is likely that the Bishop of Breslau will not remember me kindly. In his newly built and marvelously appointed house, a fine banquet awaited me in the company of a few others and there was also a short speech of welcome at the table. But I could not understand why in this city where, two months before the outbreak of World War II, I had held lectures about Thomas Aquinas to a large auditorium full of German students, I was now addressed in Polish — which had not happened in Warsaw, Lublin, and Krakow. My host, only recently in office, had, in fact, not a word of German. Beside me sat an interpreter who translated what he said. Naturally, I asked him to express my thanks for the hospitable reception, but I could not help adding the comment that the Bishop of Essen, and many a priest of his diocese, had learned Polish in order to administer the sacraments and to preach in their mother tongue to the Poles working in the Ruhr district.

When in the afternoon — in the presence of the Bishop — I was again speaking to the Breslau students, the lecture was translated for them paragraph by paragraph. I was welcomed by some of my audience — students and professors alike — with a considerable show of warmth, and in German.

Surprisingly my host from Warsaw contacted me to say that he had that same evening booked a return flight for us both. This gave me a good excuse to decline the offer of a drive around the "new Breslau," for which the Bishop was putting his car at my disposal. I had no desire for it, anyway; my friends from former years preoccupied my mind.

The next day I gave a lecture at the State University of Warsaw. It was the last one on this journey. For the first time an irritating disagreement — which could not be ironed out — prevailed in the discussion that followed the lecture. Clearly, no one was comfortable with the discussion. I was at least able to rid myself of the uneasy feeling. But that did not stop us from celebrating with a merry farewell meal as accomplices in the "half legality" of this semi-detached house — with good quantities of Bulgarian wine.

However, I was very relieved to arrive home in the evening of the following day to the freedom of the West, whatever the likewise problematic aspects it manifests — of which I am well aware.

VII

Karl Rahner — a Fragmentary Encounter

It is a strange word that Karl Rahner used as we parted company. It was tossed out in jest in a chance conversation and one which I have never been able to explain. At that time, ten years before his death, neither of us thought that we would, in fact, never meet again. But his mysterious word did, after a while, goad me into writing a rather lengthy letter — which unfortunately remained unanswered.

In the week before Palm Sunday 1972, the conference of the Ecumenical Working Group in the old Swabian monastery in Kirchberg had just ended. We were waiting outside in the street for the cars that would bring us off in our different directions as we headed home. We were chatting about this and that, and then Rahner suddenly said to me: "The fact that you visited me several times in the University Clinic in Munich I always saw as a case of 'love thy enemy'." Somewhat taken aback, I smiled and poked him in the chest. He, too, was smiling. "What sort of nonsense is that?" At this moment my car arrived. We shook hands: "See you again!" But, as I have said, this did not happen.

To the surprise of a lot of people Rahner had — after only three years — vacated the chair he had held in Munich as successor to Romano Guardini and was, in 1967, again only for a few years, my colleague at the University of Münster. It was said that an almost incurable viral sickness forced him into early retirement in 1971.

1971 was also a bad time for me and still more for my wife. For the duration of a whole winter and into the following spring we did not want to accept the failure of an operation in which she had an artificial hip joint inserted. Finally, in a new operation the hip joint — cemented in place once and for all – had to be ripped out again. And no one could or would tell us what was to happen next. So I traveled every weekend on a depressing sick-bed visit to Munich, and since Rahner's room was only a few corridors away I visited him two or three times. On one occasion I also met Joseph Ratzinger there. He had likewise been a colleague of mine in Münster, but had just moved from Tübingen to the newly founded University of Regensburg. I think it was he who brought news that Ida Görres-Coudenhove collapsed and died suddenly after a lecture to a panel of the Würzburg Synod. In our conversation we chatted away about the synod and other topical matters and, of course, not too directly about illness. It did not occur to us to start a theological debate. I don't remember ever having a real conversation with Karl Rahner. Just once, in his Münster days, he visited me in my house with a crowd of others who were congratulating me on a "round" birthday, but there was nothing more than cordial conversation.

Our first contact probably went back to the time before World War II. And, by the way: anyone who mentioned the name Rahner in those days would have been referring to his brother, Hugo Rahner. The first-edition copy — with a dedication to me — of *Geist in Welt*, which I chanced upon recently, was dated "Pullach, 9.1.48." What united us in those days was the intention formulated in this early work of "parting company with forms of 'New Scholasticism' and returning to Thomas himself." But then I could not understand that the man called shortly afterwards to a chair in Innsbruck — in a meeting which I remember clearly — tried to convince me that "today" theology could not and should not be practiced the way it was "centuries ago." I was in the process of discovering for myself the profound contemporary significance of the *Doctor Communis* of Christianity, who taught seven hundred years ago. Naturally, I knew, just as Rahner did, that it was not sufficient in interpreting Thomas to limit oneself to the *Summa*, which is a book for beginners. But the notion suggested here by Rahner that there was a "quite different" Thomas espousing a "Christian anthropocentrism" is something I was suspicious of from the beginning.

But, as I said, we were never involved in debate. The fact that we had quite different views was something we expressed with cordial irony, usually in brief comments over breakfast during the meetings of our circle. What were probably the most important differences were never aired.

I had arrived late to a meeting in the Leo Boarding School in Paderborn and it was only next morning in the chapel that I could greet different ones, in silence. A table had been set up in the chancel, and the candles for the celebration of Mass were already burning on it. But then they were extinguished again, and those on the altar at the back of the chancel were lit. The prefect of the house, as he came out of the sacristy, passed close to me and whispered that Professor Rahner was going to celebrate Mass in a completely new form. But in fact he strode to the altar, and, as in the old days, turned his back to us and celebrated a "low Mass" with an almost inaudible exchange with the altar boys. When he joined me at breakfast, I congratulated him with a smile: "Well, that was a really post-conciliar Mass!" — "But isn't that something you like as well?"

On occasion I had experienced myself how this priest, devout in his own simple and convincing way, whom I had seen walking up and down saying the Divine Office, would suddenly, in unexpected vehement non-conformism, break away from the normal; and I had often been told about it and heard it described, for example, by members of the Würzburg Synod. But it did surprise me that the protest against what had just been officially decided could be a reversion to what belonged way back in the past.

Some years previously, again in a brief conversation over breakfast, we came to speak about some controversies within the Church which in the meantime had almost been forgotten. "Given my anti-authoritarian attitude it gives me more pleasure that I bailed Schillebeeckx out of his Vatican difficulties than that I opposed Hubertus Halbfas." I had no interest in Halbfas, although perhaps in Schillebeeckx. We had met later at the Thomas Congress in Rome in 1974; to be more exact, we had seen and looked at one another, but neither of us had greeted the other. But now, at this moment, I simply could not comprehend that a man like Karl Rahner would identify himself, as if it was an obvious thing to do, with this battle-cry — anti-authoritarian — aimed in hate-filled polemic against any kind of establishment whatsoever. And I did not hide my astonishment. "We are both almost seventy years old – and you are plagued by your 'anti-authoritarian' attitude?" I don't remember what or if he replied.

Middle of March 1970. Three of us were standing in front of the Evangelical Academy in Tutzing in which the Ecumenical Work Group was starting to assemble for its first morning session. The third person apart from Rahner and me had also arrived just a few minutes ago. It was the Benedictine Victor Warnach. He was, like myself, one of the founding members of the group. Rahner had joined only later. We were all somewhat afraid of Pater Victor as a speaker because he would usually only come to the main subject of his lecture when the time allotted to him had already expired. Paul Simon's explanation for this was that, after all, the Benedictine Order was founded a few centuries before the invention of the pocket watch. For the first time in twenty-five years Pater Victor was wearing, instead of his Benedictine habit, a rather shabby civilian suit. When he approached us I deliberately expressed my amazement with exaggerated gestures. Rahner immediately turned to me in a friendly but aggressive way and defended the monk, who was looking somewhat sheepish: "Looking at you

it is not clear whether you are a professor or a lawyer or a doctor!"
I answered him in the same tone with the question which, in the
meantime, seemed to me of much more current relevance: "Is the
difference between a consecrated priest and a non-priest not much
more fundamental than the one you have just mentioned?" The
conversation broke off and the conference began. — No one had
an inkling that Victor Warnach would, exactly two months later,
be washed up dead on the beach near Rome.

On that morning Rahner and I had had a short walk behind
us. This had a particular significance. In those years there was a
Filipino Benedictine nun studying in Münster. She was a very
temperamental and highly intelligent young woman, who later did
her Ph.D. in philosophy at the Gregorian in Rome with an extremely learned dissertation on "Language Play" [Sprach-Spiel],
inspired by both Augustine and Wittgenstein. By chance, she was
also participating in Rahner's seminars and in mine; for a period
of several semesters she was a leading voice in the difficult discussions which served as a preparation for my book on love, which
had finally reached completion. She was exuberant in her devotion
to both teachers. She spent the university holidays in the General
Priory of her Order not far outside Tutzing, and when she heard
that Rahner and I would be in the Tutzing Academy for a few days
she arranged of her own accord, without asking anyone — as if it
was an obvious thing to do — that Karl Rahner would say Mass
every morning in the chapel of the religious house. Naturally, I
was to come as well and afterwards be served an excellent breakfast
in the company of a few others. On our arrival in Tutzing we found
there was already a timetable which could not be changed. And so
Rahner and I strolled out to the General Priory each morning of
the conference and celebrated the Eucharist in a contemplative
and peaceful atmosphere. Afterwards a small group gathered for
breakfast. Then we two returned happily to the Academy, deep in
thought and not inclined to converse.

At the beginning of the session on the first day a personal letter of Cardinal Döpfner was read. It was addressed to all, including the Evangelical members, inviting us to the Catholic Academy for the inaugural award of the Romano Guardini Prize and to the reception that was to follow. The recipient of the prize was Karl Rahner. We had, of course, heard about it earlier but had forgotten the exact date; and Rahner himself had not mentioned it. For the topic of his speech he had chosen a challenging topic: "Freedom and Manipulation in the Church." For better or for worse I had to stay away from the ceremonial event. I did not have the right "wedding garment"; my shoes, above all, were impossible — bright brown moccasins with thick, bright crepe soles.

The following morning — it was the last day of the conference, and Rahner had remained in Munich — I innocently asked the company at table: "So, how did it go?" They were shaking their heads, and I was given ambiguous and embarrassed answers. "It was interesting, anyway!" In private, they spoke openly, and someone said it was unfortunate. That was the kindest judgement. Some thought it an unbelievable gaffe and others said it was incredibly tactless. Rahner had even attacked the Cardinal personally — and so on. All, even his friends, and precisely his friends were disconcerted, annoyed, and disappointed.

These things were two years back in the past when I heard his farewell words about "loving your enemy." I was unable to get these words out of my head as easily as I had thought. Perhaps there was a grain of truth in them. And so I decided one day to write a letter. Since it was spontaneously written by hand I have neither a carbon copy nor a draft. But fifteen years later I know fairly accurately what was in it: naturally I realized that he had spoken in jest, and naturally I did not bear him any grudge; and yet there was something awry in it that made it impossible for me to be in agreement with him. In my memory, I told him, there were two Rahner images which did not tally with one another, and one of them was foreign to me and incomprehensible. And then I reminded him of those days in Tutzing, the untroubled cheeriness of our morning walks to the convent of the Benedictine nuns. I also wrote of what I knew about his Munich lecture, and indeed from his own well-disposed friends. I had to free myself of that by writing it to him. And since I considered I had expressed it circumspectly I was eagerly awaiting a likewise not unfriendly answer. But, as I have already said, there was no answer at all.

To mark his eightieth birthday, after which he lived less than a month, German Television carried an autobiographical retrospective spoken by Rahner himself. While I watched it and took it in, I was fascinated and thought to myself that perhaps it would have been better not to write that letter. And when a year later I visited his grave in Innsbruck, all of the disputes — which I had almost forgotten anyway — seemed simply of no consequence.

VIII
Eta Harich-Schneider

In 1986 my son sent me a death notice which had appeared in the *Süddeutsche Zeitung*: Eta Harich-Schneider died at the age of ninety-two. It was signed by a married couple (or brother and sister) whom I did not know "in the name of all relatives, friends and pupils." Then in my name too, I thought to myself. But then hardly anyone knew about our friendship; and perhaps "friendship" is too big a word. Still, after our chance meeting in September 1963, at meals in the International House in Tokyo, we saw one another many times again, in Japan and particularly later in Vienna, and got on well together. She always sat in the front row at my lectures in Tokyo and was a stimulating, attentive listener; she once brought a letter to dinner which named the five basic Confucian virtues, together with the Chinese script which belonged with them; she showed me the Catholic church in Tokyo which was difficult for a stranger to find, and in which she went to Mass every morning. There were some things which surprised me too. For example, this clearly pious Catholic gave the pert and cheerful answer to my random question as to the meaning of her double name: "The first name is my husband's; I ran away from him years ago!" It also surprised me a little how effusively the almost seventy-year-old again and again praised the beauty of a young novice, who was showing us through the extensive area of a Shinto Temple.

A few years after my return from Japan she got in touch from Vienna, where she apparently intended to live permanently. And since then, whenever I got out of the night train in the Viennese West train station, I immediately traveled to Lerchenfelder Strasse 85 as arranged. She always received me in trousers; she commented at the first visit, with complete lack of inhibition that the only table which did not shake was in her kitchen, where she had an exquisite breakfast prepared. When the alternating organizers of my lectures rang me during our long breakfast discussions, I always insisted that they invite Eta Harich-Schneider to the exclusive meals. I was already prepared for the discreet and astonished question which regularly followed about who this lady was; and I answered with the equally astonished counter-question: "Oh, you do not know Eta Harich-Schneider? In my music dictionary it says that 'she is one of the best harpsichord players of our time.' And apart from that she is professor at the Vienna School of Music." It was amazing that nobody knew her; but each time they thanked me afterwards for the enhancement of the circle through such an intelligent and vivacious partner in dialog.

At the beginning of the 70s, in her music room where we had moved for a while after the breakfast, my eye fell on a picture which I had never seen there before, but which seemed very familiar to me; I have forgotten whether it was a painting or an enlarged photograph. You saw the face of an angelically dressed girl, who was sitting between burning candles at the grand piano and playing. "I know this picture; I just don't know where I've seen it!" — "You could not know it; that is completely impossible!" But I insisted that I had seen the picture somewhere before and not just once. "Have you been to Toronto in Canada?" This question brought the memory back immediately: the picture hung in the office of the Dominican Ignatius Eschmann, the colleague of Gilson at the Institute for Medieval Studies. In 1967 I had been invited by St. Michael's College to Toronto for a few weeks when Canada was celebrating the centenary of its Dominion status. I was aware of the very early essay by Eschmann about the concept of *civitas* according to Thomas, but particularly of the work of amazing scholarship: the complete catalogue of the works of Thomas Aquinas, which Gilson had included as an appendix in his book about Thomas and which had become a classic. Of course, I visited Eschmann in the first days, and met a seriously-ill person who was in a deep depression and to whom my repeated visits appeared to give a new lease of life for a while. We even traveled together in his car an hour out of Toronto to the Jesuit novitiate and visited the famous theologian Bernard Lonergan, who was also recovering from a serious illness but had already begun to write his big work about theology and method. In St. Michael's College I was congratulated for the amazing feat of bringing Eschmann back alive from this car trip. Six months later, at Easter 1968, at the Philosophy Congress in New Orleans, to which several hundred Catholic professors of the North American continent had come, someone brought me greetings from Eschmann, whom he had met a short time previously in Toronto. A quarter of an hour later another person who had just come from Toronto informed me that Eschmann had died a few days ago.

So in his office I had seen the picture of the youthful Eta Harich-Schneider many times; after his death it had been returned to her. During the first years of Nazi rule the already well-known Professor of the Berlin State School of Music had had the Dominican, some years younger than herself, released from jail after a resolute personal appeal to the Justice Minister who was known not to be of a National Socialist cast of mind. This had earned the Minister serious criticism. I only found this out through reading the "Eyewitness reports of a traveling musician" which was published in 1978 by Ullstein under the title "Characters and Catastrophes."

This memoir was too personal for my Westphalian taste. We had a friendly-pugnacious exchange of letters which brought me a completely unexpected "other" Eta Harich-Schneider. It was hard to fathom the *coup de foudre*, the passionate love affair which was beginning with Dr. Richard Sorge, employee of the Frankfurt Institute for Social Science, correspondent for years with the Frankfurt newspaper, and at the same time Russian spy and perhaps double agent. It was he who gave Stalin the precise but not accepted information about the imminent German attack on Russia, and who let him know shortly afterwards the decisive news that the Japanese army would *not* attack Russia from the East despite their alliance with Germany; it was also he who informed the Americans about the planned attack on Pearl Harbour, and they likewise did not react. Eta Harich-Schneider describes him as the only honest, really courageous person in a corrupt and dishonest environment. The "Biographical Dictionary of German History," for the most part scientifically reliable, calls him "the idealistic leader of a large spy ring, who lived the life of a quarrelsome, bullying boozer and motorbike racer."

The love story between Richard Sorge and Eta Harich-Schneider lasted for a summer – from May until October 1941. In this month Sorge was arrested by the Japanese police and sentenced to death in a secret trial to which Germans had no access, and he was hanged on 1 July 1944. After the conclusion of the trial the prosecutor admitted that he had never met anyone in his life to compare with Richard Sorge. — I completely understand that Eta Harich-Schneider gave her autobiography the title from one of its chapters: "Spectator at the Hanging."

But I want to end my short report with something else. — After a scholarly lecture in the Düsseldorf Rhine-Westphalia Academy of Sciences, the Japanologist Bruno Lewin was sitting beside me at table. I thought of asking him whether the name Eta Harich-Schneider meant anything to him. He then laid his knife and fork on his plate and said: "You cannot ignore Eta Harich-Schneider if you want to learn about Japan properly. Her *History of Japanese*

Music is simply *the* standard work." She herself had never mentioned to me this *opus magnum* of more than seven hundred pages which had appeared in Oxford University Press in 1973. Perhaps she felt it was not worth mentioning.

IX
"He who is without sin ..."

Thankfully I have never been, as Eta Harich-Schneider calls it, "a spectator at a hanging." But in the years 1966/68, for days I attended a "war crimes trial" as an eye and ear witness at the regional court in Münster. It was about police operations in the originally Polish city of Stanislau, which in 1939 after the Hitler-Stalin pact was occupied by Russians and then in June 1941 was conquered by the German armed forces, and now belongs to Russia again. I knew one of the judges in this case very well, and he promised to let me know whenever a particularly important day in the proceedings was expected.

So one morning I entered the courtroom; a seat which had been kept for me was silently pointed out to me. The session had already started. The judge was asking the principal accused person to relate how the "whole affair" had begun. A good-looking man well able to make his point in clear, considered speech stood up. He was about five years younger than me and therefore, at the time of the crime of which he was accused, was not yet thirty-five years old. How do things like that begin? This exact question bothered me too; it still does now. And what you got to hear in the following days was certainly thought-provoking. Had I been in the same position as the police officer at that time, what would I have done myself in that barely perceptible moment when the disaster set in?

When Stanislau was taken by the German troops who were immediately pushing on further, the accused was given the assignment of forming a central police department in the conquered city. And so he had suddenly become the head of a public authority. He reported that one day a delegation of citizens appeared before him who had found their way back to some semblance of normality after the indescribable chaos of the first terrors. They pointed out to the police chief many acts of violence committed during Russian rule in the city; they added photographs of beaten-up and maltreated people, along with a list of names of the criminals; some of them had been able to flee, but most of them were still in the city and generally known. The German police authorities, who had enjoyed a considerable level of trust at the beginning, were expected to punish the guilty. "I made it clear to the people that I could not make decisions about such measures. They would have to appeal to the higher authorities in Lodz and should lodge the documents there." — "And did that happen?", asked the chairman. "Did you not do anything yourself?" — "Yes, that's what happened; and I myself waited and did nothing! It took quite a long time for news to come from Lodz. They sent me the list of names which I already knew; on it there were several names marked with an 'x'. That implied that some of the named people were to be arrested and some others were to be shot." The accused fell silent; the last part had been stated in a tone of conclusion. The following silence lasted too long for the judge and he asked sharply: "And then?" —"Then I carried out the order! I said to myself: they have investigated the matter in Lodz." — "So you arrested some and shot the others?" — "No, judge, not shot! This was an execution!" — "And what is the difference?" — "I told the condemned men what was awaiting them; and before I gave the order to shoot, I drew my sword."

Up until this moment the man had spoken without any noticeable agitation, apparently convinced of his case, and he sounded credible. I thought: assuming that he has spoken the truth, and given the same situation which was determined by the war and was difficult for the individual to comprehend, I would perhaps — even probably — not have done anything differently. But it was soon clear to me how easily in something like that, within the mechanism of a totalitarian regime, the first step can be on a path where the second step can only be avoided with difficulty, and the next steps not at all — except by virtue of an absolutely heroic decision which generally can hardly be demanded of a person. The sentence from Brecht's "Galilei" went through my head: "Unhappy the land that needs heroes."

The court case ran its course: the judge became impatient and posed the next question with blatant anger: "But later, at the mass shootings with machine guns — did you also draw your sword then? Were they also executions? Or what were they?" — Suddenly the attitude of the accused changed radically. His speech spun out of control. He spoke at first vaguely and long-windedly about things which he could not have known then, about the "Wannsee Conference" for example, at which the "final solution" of the Jewish question had been decided on. The judge interrupted him with a dismissive wave of the hand and repeated his question: "What happened then? How did you behave?" — Now, everyone knows what dreadful things happened behind the front in the East and not just there. The accused, however, had, as was proved during the course of the trial, not just carried out the orders "in the line of duty" but, in a type of rush of blood had personally been involved in horrific acts of violence of a particularly bestial kind. — This was also, as I was informed recently, the reason why a plea for clemency on the part of the man who had been condemned to life imprisonment had been denied twice. Today (1986) the condemned man, now over seventy-five-years old, is still in prison.

Later I did not attend when a whole group of accused men were standing trial. But I remember exactly a particular argument which was used several times by the main accused person: "There was nobody in Germany who stated to me clearly: what you are doing is wrong." — Again and again my thoughts went back to the borderline which is difficult to pinpoint exactly: where something can still be justified and where actual wrong begins. I still have in my ear the accused man's question, helplessly blurted out at this demarcation line. It remained unanswered and was later completely silenced: "What could I have done?"

I was reminded of all this a few weeks ago during recordings for the TV program "Witnesses of the century." Of course, among the many questions directed at me, one was certain to be asked: "When did you find out about the crimes of the Nazi Regime and how did you react to them?" — In the first volume of my autobiography which appeared in 1976, I described in detail what I had been told in my role as psychologist in the armed forces by a youthful recruit who for the first time was an eyewitness to the murder of Jews in the Ukraine. Yes, how did I react to it? I repeated what I had heard in great detail at the evening meal with my comrades who all, like me, were members of the German armed forces, in ranks of captain or major. Apart from one who loudly praised such actions as an excellent solution of the Jewish question, all remained silent. What had remained unmentioned in my book because I thought it too boastful, I did say in front of the TV camera: that at that time I said straight to the faces of my Nazi comrades that the ignominious procedures were "naked crimes"; of course, there was not a huge amount of courage attached to that. But in public I was also silent. Should I have shouted aloud: there is terrible injustice happening here? Some people did that and paid for it with their lives. Inge Scholl wrote to me shortly after the war telling me that her brother had read my books. And not until the spring of 1986 did the sister of Willi Graf, who had also belonged to the "Weiße Rose" group and had been executed, send me the photocopy of a piece of paper from her brother's diary: "Read J.P. about the Christian conception of man." This affected me in two ways. I heard this news and was ashamed. Some write things and others do them.

X
Orders, Prizes, Medals

There are also honors which make us ashamed. For that reason I did, in fact, once decline one. Fortunately, there was also another reason for declining them which seemed equally plausible.

For spontaneously saying "No" I needed not even a minute's reflection when in spring 1982 I was told by telephone that I was to be the first person to be awarded the Thomas More Medal. I have always admired Thomas More — with a feeling which combined several elements: straightforward sympathy, reverent distance, admiring enthusiasm. What I liked from the beginning was his human worldliness; his hearty, unencumbered, almost sensuous affirmation of the good things of this life; the surprising and almost disconcerting self-chastisement practiced vigorously and secretly; and, at the end, the completely amazing equanimity with which this saint climbed the scaffold: "I pray you, I pray you, Mr. Lieutenant, see me safe up and for my coming down, I can shift for myself."

No, it was simply not possible for me to accept a decoration of this kind which bore the name of a martyr. I immediately recommended someone else for the prize; and a few years later a friend I much admired received the Thomas More Medal and died shortly after. The fact that I did not want to accept it myself was my own personal choice. I would simply be ashamed. But I had another reason to hand. In the previous year, when I was being considered for the Romano Guardini Prize I had just returned from Bern, where I had received the International Balzan Prize, and people could see that I could hardly receive another distinction so soon.

I need to describe the roundabout way — likewise by telephone — by which the first notification about the Balzan Prize reached me. It was a prize I had not at all expected. — But first of all a word about another honor which I likewise, but for a totally different reason, did not accept. It was the Peter Wust Prize which was to be awarded for the first time. Perhaps there was some kind of mistake. In a Literature Lexicon it was written that I had been a very close friend of this Münster philosopher and also a successor to his chair. Neither of these things was true. Furthermore, the inner style of Peter Wust's philosophizing was—— with all due respect to his wonderful personality — so foreign to me that I was not happy to accept a distinction associated with his name. But again, I could not explicitly state that as a reason for declining. It was odd that by chance a little volume of Peter Wust's letters, published by Wilhelm Vernekohl, fell into my hands. Paging through it without much concentration I was relieved to find the dedication: "To the founder of the Peter Wust Archive at the University of Saarbrücken, Professor Joseph-François Angelloz." And so I immediately put it to the Catholic Academy in Trier that not I, but the undoubtedly deserving Frenchman was the right man to be the first recipient of the Peter Wust Prize. Since I heard nothing back it was with some trepidation that, on being invited to give a lecture, I traveled to Trier; but I was immediately greeted with the news that Professor Angelloz, now in retirement, was living in France and was delighted to accept the honor. He sent me his greetings and heartfelt thanks. I kept my thoughts to myself and did not mention that we had never met one another.

Twice, then, I succeeded in declining honors which I considered inappropriate for me. In another much more important instance I was, unfortunately, not so successful, although the circumstances were somewhat exhilarating. A few months before my seventieth birthday I heard a rumor that in honor of this occasion the intention was to confer on me an ecclesiastical Order, and I immediately asked Bishop Heinrich Tenhumberg with some urgency to make sure that this did not happen. But I was also fairly sure that he had come up with this idea himself. "From the Church I ask, as it says in the ritual of baptism, faith and the sacraments, but certainly *not* an Order." The Bishop seemed surprised, smiled, but said nothing. But I could see that he well understood my wish; after all, we had been friends for years. But then, when he rang me almost exactly a week before my birthday I knew immediately what was meant when he said that we needed "to have a talk with one another like two reasonable men." "That is no longer necessary," I said. "You already have an Order for me after all." Naturally, all he could do was confirm it, but he sounded almost apologetic. In Rome, instead of the Order they had requested something written in the Pope's hand, but the request had come too late. But, on the other hand, he said, the Order was something quite special. The document signed by the Cardinal State Secretary meant no less than my appointment as Commander of the Order of St. Gregory. But now it came about that the Bishop had to begin his birthday speech — in my family circle: my wife and children and some friends and students, all of whom knew of my often enough declared reluctance — with the admission that the Order had not yet arrived. We all answered with joyful laughter: "You see, Your Grace, it is not meant to be!"

The next day the Bishop's chaplain brought the splendid insignia in a red leather box. There was a cross with a golden band to be worn around the neck, and a large silver star to be worn on the left side of the chest: the *magnum nomisma argenteum*.

However, I was not able to decide to thank anyone for the distinction. Perhaps I should have. In any case, ten years later I took to heart the words from Cardinal Joseph Ratzinger, likewise a friend. On the occasion of my eightieth birthday I had asked him for a similar intervention. In his prompt answer he said that he was happy to do what was required, but that perhaps one should be humble enough simply to accept an Order conferred by the Church. Probably in this case an intervention would not have been necessary anyway.

The impressive jewelry of the Order of St. Gregory was photographed by my nephews at a birthday meal some days later with various kinds of lighting. Naturally, I have never worn it. Besides, as it said in the illustrated pamphlet accompanying the award, I would have to carry a sword and wear a bicorn with a white plume, and, above all, a special grey-green uniform. For me that was all going too far. As I write that down, I am reminded that I was able to use the excuse of a busy schedule in declining an invitation to the Bremen "Mariners' Meal" [Schaffermahl] — an invitation given only once in one's lifetime — as well as to the "Merchants' Meal" [Kramermahl] in Münster, whereas the main reason for declining was simply the fact that I have never owned evening attire — which I am also neither prepared to buy or to hire.

On one occasion, not having tails or a dinner jacket became a serious problem for me when accepting an award. The distinction itself was nothing particularly special, but the context chosen for the solemn conferring really was. My Spanish colleague Rafael Alvira, once a guest for some semesters in my seminars, appeared wearing a lounge suit and, to his great annoyance, had to hire a dinner jacket. I insisted, with eventual success, that my dark-grey suit with which I promised to wear a silver-grey tie, was festive enough.

At that time I found myself unexpectedly embroiled in an adventurous situation which for a time had me puzzled. In spring 1980, an Atheneo Filosofico had settled in Mexico. I had never heard of them. They told me that I had been awarded the *Premio "Doxa."* The certificate, together with the medal, was to be presented to me on 21 July in London; I was given an address which, as I found out, was difficult even for a London taxi-driver to find. To my surprise I landed into the almost week-long meeting of the "International Society for Metaphysics." Up to this point I had not known of the existence of this society, or the fact that this congress was taking place, or its theme. I was greeted in a particularly friendly way by the *Rectora* of the Atheneo Filosofico, a dainty, elegantly dressed young lady, whose dark Mexican eyes radiated an unusual lively energy. She told me something I had already gleaned from the Congress Program: that in the evening of the following day the conferring of the prize would take place in Kings College and that I was requested to make a short speech. Luckily I had to hand the English translation of a short essay on "The inevitable dilemma of a non-Christian philosophy." The dynamic *Rectora* was immediately satisfied with this topic, especially as a likely trigger for discussion. There followed, almost in passing, a conversation — which because of my firm attitude was kept short — about the dinner jacket. And so the next evening we drove to the famous college situated right by the Thames. The lift did not take us up but, instead, several floors down; under the Thames, I was thinking. Naturally, in the enormous hall only the front rows were occupied. But the Rectora, who did not at all suffer from feelings of inferiority, had arranged for no less a person than Lord Hallsbury, the President of the Royal Institute of Philosophy, to call up and introduce the award-winners. He also presented the awards, all of which bore Greek names. He put (what only looked like) a gold medal around my neck, the Premio "Doxa" with its black silk band. Rafael Alvira received the "Noesis" prize for co-editing the Philosophical Yearbook of the Universidad de Navarra. Clearly there was a slightly unreal, fantastic atmosphere surrounding this pompous ceremony in which an institute which was hardly known in Europe and, as they openly said, was only recently founded, was awarding international prizes. At the same time, my neighbor, who received the Premio "Energia," was the Rector of the University of Athens.

But enough of this! It is not my intention to antagonize my readers with an exhaustive list of awards. You get them almost inevitably if you live long enough and, naturally, with the passing of time their importance fades for the person concerned. Even the second Dr. theol. h.c. does not have the freshness and luster of the first one conferred. But sometimes certain accompanying circumstances stick in the memory more than the thing itself. For example, in 1974, when Christendom was celebrating the seven hundredth anniversary of the *Doctor Communis* Thomas Aquinas, in the city of Münster — although it has a faculty of theology and a Catholic academy — not a word about the commemoration had been communicated to the public. And so, with a certain guile I took advantage of the speech I was to make in receiving the honorary doctorate to thank, in my first sentence, the Faculty of Theology for the honor conferred on me and then, above all, for the opportunity to deliver to my revered teacher the *Laudatio* which he so richly deserved. I did that in an analysis of the concept of "creaturehood," beginning with a reference to G. K. Chesterton's suggestion of calling the last master of a still undivided Christendom "Thomas a Creatore." Afterwards a colleague in the Faculty of Philosophy, with a wink, added to his words of congratulation the dry comment: "You have converted the academic procedure very nicely into a Thomas celebration!" I took the comment as a compliment: and that was how it was intended.

There was something similar when I was surprisingly conferred with the Romano Guardini Award, which unexpectedly took me back — in a very moving way — to the beginnings of my intellectual life which had just been beginning to mature. Here there was a strange, and what I believe to be a unique, circumstance: the award, without being shared, was at the same time given to another person — Walter Dirks, a friend from way back whom I had not met for decades and who had followed a very different path from mine. A daily newspaper found this combination of prize-winners so unusual that it brought the headline "Fire and Water." As we met and shook hands on meeting at the Catholic Academy in Munich, we asked one another which of us was fire and which was water.

A particularly successful event remains in my memory precisely because the outcome was quite different from what had been planned. In 1979, on a November afternoon when it was already becoming dark, I was to receive in the town hall in Münster, as a somewhat late birthday present, the St. Paul Badge of this city which early in my life had become my home town. Originally it did not involve a public ceremony but amounted to a simple presentation in the municipal office. That suited me very well, since nothing was expected of me except a short word of thanks. What would I have spoken about? Certainly not something "philosophical." That this occasion took a different turn had to do with a visitor from Rome who unexpectedly appeared in my house. He was a theology professor from the Gregoriana who wanted to discuss business relating to a doctorate. After a while my guest commented, almost casually, that he too was from Münster — even from the same part of the city as myself. With his name — mentioned as he introduced himself — still in my ear, I asked him if his father had not been a coach-owner [Hauderer]. The name meant nothing to my children or my students. And this man who rents out horse-drawn coaches, of which he owns four or five, with as many horses — is he still alive? And he probably drives one of these coaches himself? "That's more or less right, except that it was not my father, but my grandfather." And then he mentioned the maiden name of his mother, and immediately I could see in my mind the grocer's store, just a few houses away from ours in which their beautiful black-haired daughter would often weigh sugar and flour for us. "Yes, my mother was a beautiful woman, even in her old age." And so this internationally known theologian had his roots in a part of town where simple folk lived — like ourselves: the primary school teacher with his wife from the village and his five children. In our conversation, which could have gone on forever, we reminded one another of people we knew — one of us more than the other — in our neighborhood. There was, for example, the master cobbler who sang as he worked and whose gifted son was not to become a cobbler. He had him trained as a pianist, from whose music-loving family — as we both knew from hearsay — the General Music Director of a big German city was to emerge. And just around the next corner there was the master painter whose eldest son, with his rich, resounding bass voice, was already making his mark in the Cathedral choir and went on to become an opera singer and had sung, until his early death, the role of Osmin in Mozart's *Il Seraglio* in numerous German theaters. The younger brother had become a painter, who some years ago was given the title of Professor by the Minister for Culture in Stuttgart.

During all of this, the thought occurred to me that, on receiving the St. Paul badge, I should relate all these things which I had witnessed at first hand during my boyhood years. I intended in this way to honor and to express my gratitude to the preceding generation. And so, just before the event I told the chief Municipal Director, whom I knew very well, that I would not limit myself to the pre-arranged brief word of thanks but that for my answer I needed about half an hour. It then obviously turned out that it was still possible to give the event some publicity. The guests — a respectable number — were shown into the "armory" immediately above the room where peace was declared in 1648 at the end of the Thirty Years War. In the haste, no chairs or even a lectern had been provided, and after the Lord Mayor's laudatory speech I told my true stories to all the people as they stood around. Everyone immediately understood that these were intended as stories with a "moral." The idea was to show what these simple folk, our fathers and mothers, who had never had such a thing as a holiday in Mallorca and whose almost daily midday dinner was stew, paid in order that their children could do more than just make money. They paid with their unquestioning frugality, their uncomplaining, untiring self-sacrifice and the neglect of their own needs. I wanted, above all, to make clear that it is precisely from these types of people that a nation really lives, and to whom the fine words of the German Jew, Walter Benjamin, apply: "Honor without fame/Greatness without glitter/Dignity without pay." Benjamin used these words in introducing his memorial book about "German People" [Deutsche Menschen].

The Balzan Prize is linked in my memory with particularly unusual accompanying circumstances. Before this story began I had hardly heard of the award. It began with a letter I received from a young Italian university lecturer in Turin. We were conversing for a moment at the crowded reception to which the Italian State President had invited the Thomas Congress in 1974 in the Quirinal Palace. He had been looking for me. Of course, I hardly managed to say a word since, in his exuberant but quite knowledgeable appraisal of my *opuscula*, which had been published in Brescia, there was no interrupting him. After a few minutes we were already separated. So it was from this young Italian that, much later, I received a letter. In his minuscule, scarcely legible handwriting, the letter contained a strange but insistent request that I send to the address of the Philosophy Professor Vittorio Mathieu — likewise teaching at the University of Turin — a *curriculum vitae* and a list of my publications and, above all, a list of all the awards and distinctions I had received so far. It would be better, he wrote, not to mention the recent invitation to the *Pontificia Accademia Romana di San Tommaso d'Aquino.* He said further that he was writing about the conferring of an award of I cannot remember how many million Italian Lire. How strange, I thought, and I sent off the requested documentation to the colleague in Turin who was completely unknown to me. I did not really doubt the seriousness of the thing, although I was somewhat disconcerted. I soon received a letter of thanks and confirmation, and here for the first time there was mention of the Balzan Prize. At the same time Professor Mathieu told me, deeply moved, of the sudden death of the young lecturer, obviously a close friend, who had lost his life in a traffic accident. It seemed to me a sad and mysterious "coincidence" that this friendly intermediary vanished from the scene once his task had been carried out. It made me ponder.

Professor Mathieu had added a somewhat problematic postscript to his letter: namely, the question whether I could have the Düsseldorf *Akademie der Wissenschaften*, of which I am a member, provide him with a letter of recommendation in my favor. It was immediately clear to me that I could not and would not do it. But after a while a university colleague who had influence in the Academy spontaneously declared his willingness to make the recommendation. But understandably he was told that the Academy could not accede to such a vague request in the desired form.

In the meantime I had found out more about the Balzan Prize — for example, that the award amounted to 250,000 Swiss francs; that it was presented in alternate years in Rome and Bern by the Head of State, and that the winner was selected by an international jury drawn from all European countries. I did not know a single jury member personally. My Turin colleague probably was one of them. Months passed since my last contact with him, so, for better or for worse I let the matter rest, and finally I almost completely forgot about it.

Then suddenly everything happened very quickly. In November 1981, as I was about to give my evening lecture of that semester on the "Current Relevance of Scholasticism," I was confronted at the open door of my house by an excited neighbor who handed me a note with an out-of-town telephone number written on it which I was to ring immediately. It was very important, she had been told. Although I already had my coat on, I went back inside to the telephone on my writing table. The *Bild*-Editors in Essen answered the phone: Did I know that I had been awarded the Balzan Prize? — at least, that is what the "dpa" had found out at a conference in Milan. "Did you reckon on this? Are you surprised?" — "Yes, of course I am surprised! After all, Pope John XIII and Mother Teresa won the prize!" — When I returned from my lecture there was a telegram from Professor Mathieu awaiting me in confirmation of the news. But the earliest announcement in the German press was in that tabloid, together with my surprised reaction and a calculation of the prize money in German Marks.

When at the end of February in the following year I arrived in Bern with my son for the presentation of the award, although tired from the long train journey I was whisked away from Hotel Reception to a press conference which had already started. The prize-winners — besides myself, a French lawyer and three English geologists — had to face the questions of a highly intelligent and well-prepared moderator who was clearly representing the Balzan Foundation, and some journalists. One of them wanted to know how I was thinking of using the considerable money involved. The British geologists, all three of them quite young, tried, with some embarrassment, to answer. The question was immediately passed on to me and my immediate answer ("No comment!") was met with good-natured laughter. During this whole evening the mood was good. When I greeted the President of the Swiss "Fondo," a Zurich banker, using his appropriate title, this man, who looked like a respectable and prosperous farmer, said: "Don't say 'President'! I'm the cashbox!" And when he invited us to an evening meal he said in all simplicity that the restaurant he had chosen had the best chef in Switzerland. Before the meal, which was a relaxed and cheerful event, with cocktail glass in hand I finally got to know my charming Turin colleague, Professor Mathieu, and also some other members of the jury — for example, Sir Bernard Katz, who had been awarded the Nobel Prize for Medicine in 1970. With natural simplicity, this Jewish emigrant spoke about his university years in Leipzig, his city of birth; just recently, on a visit to Berlin, he had been asked to recite in Saxon dialect the apparently much talked-about poem about "little red blood cells." Here he did it again at my request. Besides, he was the person who pointed out to me that I was the first German Balzan Prize winner. When I mentioned that Paul Hindemith and Karl von Frisch were also Award Winners, the answer came promptly that in 1962 Hindemith had been an American citizen for many years and that Karl von Frisch was an Austrian!"

My siblings and some friends had arrived for the especially solemn celebration of the ceremony in the Great Council Room of the Bern canton to be held on the following morning. My son and I were almost the last to leave the Town Hall and to set out for the midday meal in the Hotel Bellevue. As we left, a woman we did not know was going the same way and joined us. I asked whether she had anything to do with the Balzan Award and was somewhat surprised to hear that she was a niece of Balzan himself. We found out more about the bearer of this name: for example, that he had emigrated from Mussolini's Italy and had left the enormous wealth he had afterwards accumulated in Switzerland to the daughter who was born to him *extra muros*, as our companion described it, and that she then, for her part, had become the donor of the prize — something which only careful scrutiny of the discreet official version would reveal.

Arriving home after all this I could at last, at my leisure, read the gold lettering written on the parchment. I was especially pleased to see that the reason for the award, as I could now see for the first time, was precisely what had always been my greatest concern: namely, expressing myself in comprehensible, non-specialized

155

language "which was capable of awakening for a world-wide public a philosophical awareness of the ultimate questions about human existence." And no matter how much it may seem like self-praise, I am not ashamed to say it.

XI
My Imposter

Sometimes we think we are cleverer than we are. But we are quite ashamed to name the price we have had to pay for this mistake.

When my great-uncle, a priest, was approached by someone asking for money and aiming to set the mood by saying "Praise be to Jesus Christ," he would confuse him by answering: "Good morning! How's it going?" But no one ever left his country parish house empty-handed. The same kind of unsentimental generosity was also customary in my parents' house. This continued in me with the feeling of a natural obligation not to turn anyone away who knocked on the door looking for help. I never believed it when people said that in our country no one needed to beg. But I did soon follow the advice of some friends experienced in the social charitable sector who said never to give cash that would immediately be converted into alcohol. But I found that this, too, can be necessary from time to time — but also André Gide's profound entry in his diary should also be kept in mind: "That one can never be drunk enough." And so these "homeless" people who used simply to be called "beggars" (but the word does not quite apply to the mostly well-clothed men; and they are, by the way, mostly men and seldom women), were given a docket to be exchanged for food in a supermarket. On the docket are the words: "No spirits," a requirement which was probably not very effective.

Naturally, word got around very quickly, and soon, in the course of a month, more than twenty regulars appeared at my door, sometimes in twos or threes. They did not enter the house. They stayed outside and chatted about this and that and soon went off with their docket. Sometimes there were also "problems." For instance, someone said he could no longer go into a particular store. "Why not?" — "Because the detective comes and throws me out." There was no need to ask any further questions, and my decision not to give cash was beginning to weaken — for a moment, anyway. One of my regulars was referred to as the "murderer"; he had a long prison sentence behind him and now, as his comrades told me, he lived in fear of "revenge." The Eumenides are alive and well. — Sometimes a "new" one appeared, wishing to discuss his particular case with me. I would bring him into the house and into my study — something against which my friends were constantly warning me. He had recently been released from prison, and one of my dockets would be of little use to him. The story you are about to hear is one you know before the visitor begins to speak. So I once interrupted a young fellow as he approached my desk. "Don't say anything. I think I already know what you are going to tell me: you are just out of prison, you have a girl-friend who is pregnant; you have found an apartment but you don't have the money for paying rent in advance or for the deposit. True?" Exactly, came the answer. He produced from his pocket an already filled-out rental agreement and put it on the table in front of me. Quite impressed with the accuracy of my casually thrown out diagnosis, I cast a fleeting glance over the contract and handed it back to him with a shake of the head. A deposit of five hundred Marks is required. "You don't think I'm going to make you a present of so much money?" Clearly this did not sound as if it was my last word. And when my visitor, almost in shock, assured me that I was not to give him a present of anything, not even a penny; that he had the prospect of some great "black labor" and the whole sum would be paid back very soon — I wrote him, with hardly any hesitation, an IOU and put a 500 Mark note on the table. After he had signed he made the casual comment that the "e" in his name "Graefe" is really a lengthening "e"; "but we always say Jürgen Gräfe." Not exactly uneducated, I thought, is this twenty-seven-year-old, who now went away happy. As for myself, I was not yet aware that I had just paid the first instalment of the penalty demanded of a person who thinks he is the cleverer one — without being it. Just a few days later Jürgen Graefe was on the telephone: he had found a particularly good job opportunity with a sub-contractor; the only thing is that he had to travel to Munich for the job and he needed more money for this. A half an hour later he was again standing at my writing table; for "proper order" he presented evidence of the rail fare as provided at the railway station and, for better or for worse, I gave him money for the fare. As I was writing out the new IOU I asked him how he had found my private telephone number. A certain Denkmann had given it to him. "And who is that?" "A failed theology student, I think." When a short time later I asked our parish priest about the name he looked at me in puzzlement: "Who doesn't know the name Denkmann?" Well, I, at any rate, had never heard the name. But at least amongst Church people his name was not unfamiliar. The Mother Superior of a convent called him "a shining light in the boozing fraternity"; he was occasionally to be seen working as a cleaner in the cathedral. She said I had changed his name slightly. The name "Jürgen Graefe" was a false name; I would find out only later that the fellow who used the name in signing the IOUs was not named Jürgen Graefe at all.

And so Jürgen Graefe, or whatever his real name was, announced that he was back "from Munich" surprisingly early; the "sub-contractor" shamefully deceived him. Now a new problem: the previous tenant, whose furniture they had naturally taken over although it had not been fully paid for, was sitting in the apartment and was not going to shift until he had his money. And so the fellow was standing in front of my table again; and while I was writing him a new IOU he told me he had only been released on probation and had to report regularly to the police. Again he assured me that I would soon be getting my money back, every cent of it. His reasoning was somewhat cheering: he had not been imprisoned for property theft but for bodily harm — for which reason he had to pay compensation in instalments. Using such cleverly interwoven casual statements he managed again and again to persuade me to "lend" him money. He was always inventing new, sometimes bizarre and yet not totally improbable crises; once even his girlfriend had been abducted as a hostage for blackmailing him to pay money he owed and which I, of course, provided.

But suddenly he took it too far. Within my circle of friends we were already deliberating on ways of providing special help for when the child they were expecting was born. Here Jürgen Graefe made a mistake from which there was no way back. As usual, after a telephone call he arrived in the house one evening worked up and distraught. He had been taken into custody for twenty-four hours and the next day he was to lodge a particular sum of money with the court. And so, a new IOU. When I asked where he had been locked up the answer came promptly: "At Garden Street, naturally"— i.e., in the prison which in our town is still called "the Jail." The information, thrown like that back over his shoulder, sounded light-hearted and almost cheeky. But then, as he went down the steps somewhat hesitantly and into the street, I could see by him that he knew: "I got that wrong!"

In fact, I found out next day from the prison that there was no such thing as a twenty-four hour imprisonment, and the name Jürgen Graefe was not known either to the court cashier's office or to the police — where they immediately put me through to the clerk. The official heard my report without interposing any questions and then said, with philosophical calmness, that people are bad; but he was surprised at my almost inexcusable gullibility. Naturally he could not know that, infuriatingly, it had to do with the false security of someone who thinks he knows better. I then asked what was to happen now. "If you don't make a report nothing happens." And so I wrote a brief report and sent it to the police station. A few days later I heard the same voice again — sufficiently familiar to me by now — and he gave the false name. I said I was only prepared to speak when the repayments began, and I hung up. But the phone rang again, and it was the same voice; he clearly had the need to "confess": he had had to lie, otherwise he would not have been given the money — and he had a pressing need for it. But when I asked him his real name there was silence.

Meanwhile I had found out that that "failed theology student," the "shining light of the boozing fraternity," was overnighting in one of the Caritas houses for the homeless, and I told him he was not to pass on my telephone number to imposters. His reply was perfect in its form, an almost preciously formulated typed letter ("I am distressed to read ..."); also, he had never heard the name Jürgen Graefe.

For some time I heard nothing further. But the story is not yet finished.

"Will you give me a couple of hundred Mark notes if I come to your door?" This is the question which surprised me one morning in a telephone call from an obviously good-humored man, who then gave his name and his occupation: detective superintendent in charge of "fraud cases." My report had landed on his table, but there was not much he could do with it. Above all, there was no personal description: how tall, how old, hair color, glasses? — he needed to know all that; besides, he needed the IOUs with the signatures; above all, what was missing from my report was the final sentence: I hereby file a demand for prosecution. Now, I had only kept the last of the IOUs with the sum total – and which I am not prepared to mention here. But: demand for prosecution? In prison young people *really* become damaged. "Perhaps," said my superintendent, "but we can't just simply let them run around." — And so

I wrote down everything I could remember, and I finally agreed to the demand for prosecution. At the same time I was fairly convinced that they would never catch up with Jürgen Graefe. But lo and behold! — not long afterwards the superintendent summoned me to a line-up. He was even prepared to bring me to the police station in his car. But it would be distasteful for me to meet the fellow again. "But he won't see *you*; you will see *him*. Have you never heard of the Venetian mirror?" Looking through the mirror — a kind as yet unknown to me — I saw seven or eight men standing in a line, each of them holding up a number. After a while I said: "It is the man with the number five." I did not realize as yet that I, too, was being tested. Only when I was required to look a second time did I notice that the numbers had in the meantime been switched. I also only learned afterwards that all of these men, apart from the suspect, were harmless employees of the police station. In any case, I knew the suspect the first time. The second time, different lighting was used and my eyesight, weakened since my cataract operation, made me uncertain. I was not able to decide. This would have further consequences. — Brought back home in the car, I paged through an album with thirty or forty photos which the superintendent put in front of me. He was meanwhile making notes. Finally I put my finger on a particular image; silently, the superintendent took note. Some pages later I thought the same man was there but with an entirely different haircut. The superintendent confirmed to me not only that both photos were of the same man, though a few years apart, but also that they were photos of the man I had just identified. However, all of this was not enough. They were going to present a handwriting sample to an expert graphologist. "But you have only the one signature." "Then he is going to write something more." I mentioned that there was another witness, a young sculptress who, by chance, had been visiting me and had seen him through the door for a few minutes; since she could make a portrait of him from memory I was confident that she would recognize him with certainty. Her telephone number and address were written down. The photo album was put in front of her, but unfortunately in her attempts at identification she wavered between two photos; still, one of them was a photo of my Jürgen Graefe. She was, however, also able to mention a doctor familiar with the drug scene who also knew the name Jürgen Graefe. But the superintendent dismissed this with the gesture of someone who has superior knowledge: "We are dealing with four people who use this name, but it is not the real name of any of them."

After a long gap in which nothing seemed to be happening I again received an unexpected visit from the superintendent. Casually, he showed me the now voluminous documents. "We haven't been idle!" He had also investigated the "shining light" amongst the sleepers without any significant result; "a harmless crank." The main person, whose name was mentioned almost inadvertently, was a difficult case, more difficult than expected. He was at present in jail: "Drugs!" So it was true. But he was refusing to write anything on paper. "And you can't force him to do it? And a letter written from prison — which is censored in any case — you can't give that to a graphologist?" "No, that's not possible." So it was clear that we lived in a constitutional state.

But the story is not yet finished. In the summer of 1987 I was summoned as a witness in the case against a man behind whose name I suspected I would find my imposter. And in fact I see in the dock "Jürgen Graefe" beside the young defense lawyer. She must have advised him to say he had never seen me before. I looked at him straight in the face: "We know one another very well." His expression remained unchanged. Besides me there was another witness: Denkmann, the "shining light." While we were waiting outside I had to fend off energetically the intrusive garrulousness of this crazy fellow. I was turning away without speaking when from his pocket he hastily produced a set of rosary beads which he said — and it was probably true — he had received from the Pope himself. What he had to say was of no significance for the trial. The result was, as I heard a few days later: one year in prison without probation.

My assumption that this was now over proved to be premature. The defense had obtained an appeal hearing, claiming that because of my poor eyesight I was incapable of identifying the accused. And so after a few weeks there were new proceedings, this time before the regional court. The clever presiding judge asked me to describe the face of the two persons sitting either side of him and then asked me about the color of the pencil he was holding in his hand. Thanks to the perfection of the glasses from Zeiss the issue under discussion was quickly clarified. The appeal was thrown out, and the judgment was upheld.

Deep in thought, and without any sense of satisfaction, I went out into the rain.

XII
A Gentlemen's Evening

The Intercity train coming from Cologne stopped just before reaching the station in Duisburg. In a reassuring announcement we were asked for our understanding: at the station in Duisburg there was a breakdown which would soon be fixed. But then we waited for almost an hour, and in Duisburg police searched every compartment. "Bomb scare!" But nothing was found. In my compartment, besides me there were two military officers — obviously high-ranking, to judge by the gleaming silver on their epaulettes. The unusual event initiated a conversation. After a while, in an answer to my question I learned that one of them belonged to the air force. I put his age at mid-fifties, and so in the last war as a thirteen-year-old he would have been too young even to be an anti-aircraft assistant.

In this summer of 1987 I was gathering thoughts relating to a particular chapter of my autobiography. The subject of the chapter is "A Gentlemen's Evening" to which I was invited and for which I was asked by the Commander of the Luftwaffe Group North in Münster to speak on a theme of general interest. I then landed, quite unexpectedly, into an unusual conversation group. That was about twenty-five years ago. And the thought came to me to ask my Luftwaffe officer traveling with me whether the surname "Student" meant anything to him — the name of the Luftwaffe officer Student. My neighbor looked out the window and repeated the name to himself several times; the name said nothing to him. So

I named a couple of possible clues: parachute troop, Holland, Crete. He seemed to be vaguely remembering something, but he said immediately: "In our training, you must remember, the theme 'German Luftwaffe in World War II' was taboo." Here again, I thought, is confirmation of the words of my teacher Thomas Aquinas with their manifold implications: "Praise of bravery depends on justice." The most daring, most intelligent, most dangerous undertakings by soldiers — which are often associated with extreme willingness to make sacrifices — cannot simply be praised when they are performed in the service of a criminal power; but it would be no less false to condemn them summarily and without distinction as likewise criminal; and with regard to the decision to keep silent about these things: it is indeed understandable and possibly even deserving of respect; but it can also thwart the inner cleansing, the catharsis, through which this tragedy, too, could perhaps make even these awful events fruitful.

Naturally, I counted it an honor to address the gathering of officers of this great command. On the other hand, I knew from experience that such officially arranged cultural events do not usually produce the crackling atmosphere of spontaneous attention that a lecturer desires. After a brief word of thanks the Commander, whom I had been sitting next to, led me — amidst the measured, polite applause I had expected from the auditorium — past the uniformed men to a table occupied exclusively by civilians, in whose company I was to spend the rest of the evening. The formal introductions were brief and I caught not a single name. After a while it became clear that all were high-ranking retired Luftwaffe officers whose civilian suits did not sit quite right with them. Probably, looking at me they could see I had never been a proper soldier. To avoid all misunderstanding I "confessed" straight away that I had served for a few years in the army psychological service. At the table there were some who were born in the previous century and were therefore seventy years old or more; and understandably they showed their skepticism about the "psychological" selection process which had remained unfamiliar to them. Their hostility was almost tangible and I decided, somewhat mischievously, to go on the offensive — with the markedly casual comment that the Luftwaffe had precisely this process to thank for one of its most successful and most highly decorated fighter pilots. Naturally, they wanted me to explain. So I told the story of Werner Mölders, who, had it not been for the human understanding of a bright and courageous military psychologist, would not even have been admitted into the training course for pilots. Not without a certain edge in his voice, my neighbor on my left-hand side — somewhat younger than the others at the table — said that he knew Mölders had been characterized by the psychologists as only "conditionally suitable." I admitted this. "True. But it is less than half the truth. The point lies elsewhere." It was noticed that my neighbor's words had surprised me. They were all looking at me. But my powder was still dry. So I calmly continued my story — that, because Mölders had completely failed some of the tests, the psychologist had the right, in accordance with the rules of the examination procedure, simply to end the process right there. "But that is precisely what he did not do! He was convinced that this unusual examinee would be man enough to overcome his functional deficits, and so he was daring enough to pronounce him "conditionally suitable" and in this way at least to keep open the path to his training as a pilot. — Later there were some further difficulties for Mölders; the change of instructor, for example, which occurred quite seldom and was problematic. But finally the impossible came to pass: the "conditionally suitable" became the most successful German fighter pilot. Our fundamental enemies in the National Socialist Party did not hesitate to hurl Mölders's examination documents onto the Air Marshal's desk, with the result that in 1942, in the middle of the war, the whole Luftwaffe psychology operation was abolished from one day to the next.

The men around the table had listened with rapt attention. This was all new to everyone — except for the neighbor on my left. He was on fire to introduce another new topic; but here, too, it emerged that he had only half of the truth. There is another case, he said, of a highly decorated fighter pilot who had likewise been disqualified by the psychologists; and he immediately gave the name which, as then became clear, was known to all (but is not to be revealed here). Naturally, I could only confirm what my neighbor said. But then I immediately spoke of the completely different reason for this "disqualification," which, of course, did not at all bar his way into pilot training. The reason was unreliability. "He was a greyhound!" One of them, booming, banged on the table: "That's what he was, and that's what he is today!" General laughter. But he was of no further interest to the group around the table. However, Mölders was still interesting — and what became of him later. The conversation raged back and forth. Unfortunately, I could never tell who was speaking. One of them said that Mölders's death in a crash was a mysterious affair; it had never been cleared up. — No, another one contradicted, there was nothing devilish at work; that has been established in the meantime; yet, on the other hand, it is puzzling how a pilot would fly into a chimney. — But in any case it was clear to all that Mölders was not involved with the Party. He was a good Catholic! But that did not stop him from fighting in the secret Condor Legion against Catholic Spain. But still he did risk, when being solemnly conferred with the diamonds of the Knight's Cross, answering Hitler's question whether he had a particular wish by saying, loudly and clearly, that he wished no harm would come to the Bishop of Münster. That is what Mölders himself told a comrade. That was in the summer of 1941 after Bishop von Galen held his famous sermons against the murder of the mentally ill. Hitler said in response, according to Mölders, "Nothing will happen to him." All right, but you don't kill a successful fighter pilot and then immediately give him a State funeral!

– Many things are possible. In any case, we know that immediately after the crash Mölders's home was searched. – Unbelievably, during this fateful flight he was on his way to a State funeral; and this pompous act was also a lie! — You can't say that! Such a popular figure as Ernst Udet richly deserved a State funeral! — At the same time, it was a lie that he died as a result of a tragic accident; but naturally that is what was widely believed. — Was he therefore not "The Devil's General"? — No! Zuckmayer's play is superb, but it has nothing to do with Ernst Udet. Udet had long since been written off. He is supposed to have been responsible for the failure of the England campaign. He was disappointed, became morose, started to drink; and finally he shot himself in the head.

I was fascinated as I listened in silence to this noisy conversation, fired more and more by alcohol. The table companion at my left seemed to want me to speak again and asked about the "equipment" for our investigations which we could only use in the rooms of the duty office. It was clear that no one at the table was interested in such things, and besides, I did not like the ironic tone of the question about "equipment." I therefore only took up his reference to our investigations and spoke about the tours we made to the changing locations of the troops. For example, soon after the occupation of Holland we were detailed to visit a unit on the coast and would have passed Rotterdam. "For the first time — the air attack had taken place three or four months previously — we saw with our own eyes a city in ruins. We drove along the streets, which by now had been repaired, passing by the open cellars which had been completely cleared out. The sight left us all speechless. No one said a word." With this innocently initiated report I had, without realizing it, touched a wound which had not yet been completely healed after nearly twenty-five years. "If you knew," said a voice interrupting me in extreme excitement, "how desperately I tried with radio signals, unsuccessfully, to hold up and divert the bombers flying in from around Bremen! The mere thought of it makes me feel sick even today. Attacking Rotterdam had become superfluous. It made no sense! The Dutch capitulation had been achieved at the very moment the bombing began!" — Another man added in a consciously calm voice that the attack had, in fact, been postponed; but for incomprehensible reasons the flight start began an hour earlier than ordered and planned; some mistake had been made at headquarters. Naturally, I said nothing further. There was a slightly uncomfortable pause. The "Rotterdam" theme was obviously exhausted. A sip or two of wine was taken. For a moment some looked across to the man sitting opposite me who seemed to be the oldest of the group. It was as if they were waiting for him to say something. But he remained silent — in a decided, but not unfriendly way. I, too, looked at him. Then suddenly the thought came to me to ask him a question.

On his lapel I had noticed a strangely shaped badge of white enamel; it reminded me of something I knew quite well – but what that was would just not come to me. But suddenly I knew. The badge had the shape of the island of Crete, which my wife and I had visited the previous summer.

Immediately it was clear to me that the man opposite me could only be General Student. And so I asked him why he was wearing an image of the island of the minotaur on his lapel. In a flash the face which until now had looked so serious brightened up with a smile, and it was with obvious pleasure that this man, who had been so steadfastly silent, now related in detail how, in May 1941, he and his paratroopers had to engage in battle with the New Zealanders who were the most extremely tough opponents right to the end. But after the war a group of New Zealand Crete veterans formed a club and elected him as their Honorary President. After a few moments of reflection, he added, with a touch of bitterness: "This is the only war decoration that I constantly wear."

But, at a stroke, this newly-told story changed the atmosphere at our table. There had been peals of laughter, but until now there had been no trace of a friendly smile on the faces. After a while, in good humor we shook hands and left.

As for myself, I went home somewhat depressed and sad. The burden of our destructive history, which was still with me under the surface, had revealed itself to me only too clearly. On that evening in February 1964 I had known very little. The more important things I found out only later. That General Student, a fifty-year-old, had parachuted into "Holland" with his unit was common knowledge to everyone. But I was probably the only one at the table who did not know that they had landed on the outskirts of Rotterdam; that some of his troops were surrounded and in grave danger of being wiped out; that, understandably, no one must have been more interested than General Student in preventing, by all possible means, the postponement of the air attack and, by the same token, the ending of hostilities; and that, just before the bombing of Rotterdam, Student suffered a serious head wound. Above all, at this time I did not yet know other things that happened after the war. The planner and leader of the attack on Crete, which was daring and had an unusually high rate of casualties, did not only receive the chivalrous distinction from his New Zealand foes; it also happened that a British General, acting as a judge in court, absolutely refused to confirm — and thereby prevented — the sentence of five-year imprisonment passed by the victors' military tribunal against the enemy for alleged crimes. And in a well-documented publication of the Freiburg Military History Research Institute in 1982 I read that General Student, condemned to death by a French military court, then first had his sentence commuted to life imprisonment and later passed some time in humiliating circumstances in a prison.

There was no mention of all of that at table on that evening. And although perhaps no one had anything to hide, General Student was probably not the only one who remained silent about what he had done and what had happened to him. — But for the younger officers, who had still been sitting there together quite at ease, the deeds and experiences of the German Luftwaffe in World War II were, as I had learned recently, "quite taboo."

XIII
The Chauvinist

"Poitiers! Well, what was with Poitiers? Didn't something special happen there?" At this moment my wife was, of course, not thinking of the battle of Poitiers in which Charles Martel defeated the Arabs. No, we were relaxing, paging through a photo album and recalling the car trips we made with our friend Dr. Schranz, who, in the early '50s, drove us all over France for weeks on end, during which time we visited innumerable — mainly Romanesque — churches and monasteries, many of them quite unknown. Now, of course, twenty-five years later, such a journey would be unthinkable. Our friend had died in 1961, and my wife had been in hospital for some weeks after an operation which, as would soon become clear, was only apparently successful. And so we were looking with astonishment and joy at the photos we had taken. And again the old truth was confirmed, according to which what has been seen and experienced with attention will take on a quite new significance in the light of memory.

In the glorious month of September in the summer of 1954 we were driving from Bourges on the way to Poitiers. The "special" thing my wife referred to in her question did not really happen in Poitiers itself, but on the way there. I turned back a few pages in the album and showed her a poorly exposed photo on which we could see our friend, turned to one side in thought, and herself, but also the feet and trousers of a man who was lying on his back under our car. And now she remembered immediately. There really was something special — even disturbing — about this man under the car.

A few kilometers short of Poitiers we made a stop in the country at Chauvigny. The helpful Michelin Guide to the "Beautiful Churches of France" referred to the Romanesque church of the village, typical of Poitou, as "interesting" and the capitals as "unusually beautiful"; and the church was, indeed, worth the short visit. As we were driving away, some people who happened to be passing made signs to us with some excitement, pointing to something behind our car; we stopped and saw on the road a small trail of leaking petrol. A boy brought us what looked like the broken-off head of a bolt that must have been knocked off the tank when the car collided with the raised stones skirting the footpath. Our friend Dr. Schranz temporarily replaced the bolt, and we drove to a small café, clearly the only hotel in the village. The door was wide open and we inquired about a gas station or garage. The people shrugged — there was little hope of anything happening on a Sunday afternoon. But they did tell us about a garage that might possibly be open just outside the village. But it was closed; and so, at a loss, we returned to the café. And then, quite unexpectedly, the story which has remained mysterious to us right down to the present day began to unfold. Out of the café came a wiry man of about forty, dressed not without a certain elegance. He approached us at the car and asked in perfect German: "What's the problem?" When we explained to him that a screw had come loose from the petrol tank and had only been provisionally put back, there came the very definite reply which sounded somewhat like a rebuke that there is no such thing as a screw in the tank, but rather a bolt that was welded in. With obvious impatience he listened to the Doctor's explanations for a while and then quickly strode back into the café. A minute later he came out to us again, and as he drew on his fashionable gloves he informed us – again in his very definite manner — that he would fix the problem himself. Then he pointed

174

to the only car parked in front of the café and said, almost in the tone of an order, that we were to follow him. He got into his car and drove off. We looked at one another, taken aback, and did in fact follow him. What else were we to do? And where, and how far out of Chauvigny were we to travel? We drove out into the open countryside where there were no houses in sight until we came to a narrow road leading off the main road, past a kind of gate-house, into the spacious courtyard of a large farm. We stopped and climbed out. The stranger casually commented that it was almost a miracle that our tank was not completely empty by now. Then he disappeared through the gate of a stable; he said, speaking to us back over his shoulder, that he would have to change his clothes. Wearing an elegant pair of overalls and swinging a bucket in his hand he first of all drained off the amazingly large amount of fuel. In the neighborhood, he told us curtly, there was a young friend of his, a laborer; he would weld the bolt back into place, even on a Sunday. Then he skillfully pulled himself under the car, expertly removed the tank, stowed it in his car and hurtled off. There had been no time for a conversation, so that we did not even know the man's name, no more than he knew ours. For the time being, on the basis of the village being named Chauvigny, it occurred to us to give him the crazy name "Chauvinist." Nothing stirred in the rather stately farmhouse, although it was not unoccupied. There seemed to be an almost ghostly silence about it. Darkness was gradually setting in and it was becoming cold. I brought my wife her coat from the car. We waited for a good hour; we were wondering, rather anxiously, how this was going to develop. And then the familiar car rolled back into the courtyard. The tank, half-filled again, had indeed been repaired, and was silently built back into the car. And then our man crawled out from under the car: "Done!" Relieved, we thanked him and asked what we owed him. He dismissed the question: "You are going to Poitiers? Invite me to a meal. I'll follow you in the car." And that is exactly what happened.

During the meal we finally asked this mysterious helper, who, by the way, still did not reveal his name, why on earth he had taken on all this hardship. "Out of sheer boredom!" This rather brusque answer at first gave the impression that he was resolved to say nothing further. But then — he drank his glass of red wine nearly always with one swallow, and many times a freshly filled carafe was put on the table — we were gradually able to put together the fragments of a story which almost made us forget Romanesque architecture. At a stroke, the story brought us back to the period in which we were actually living: the not yet completed first decade after World War II. Naturally we already knew that we were sharing a meal with a German national who felt the need to speak again with people who spoke his mother tongue. But then it emerged that it was impossible for him to return to Germany; nor did he want to anymore. Why was he not able to? We asked no questions. But soon, in a rather casual way it became clear that this former SS man would have his reasons. And there was not a word of explanation about how and when and on the basis of what he was able to find this hiding place in this remote farm. But nothing prevented us from asking quite naturally why he was so incredibly bored. He emptied his glass again with one long draught, gave a side-long glance, and said full of rage: "Because my girlfriend is not here! She has gone away, although she didn't want to. But she had to accompany her mother as a precaution." We then heard that the girl's father, the owner of the property, had died some years previously. He had, by the way, been a French officer. And since then this man had "managed things." The widow had been completely at the mercy of the merchants. For example, no one checked whether the amount of coke stated on the bill was actually delivered into the cellar. But now all that had changed. And naturally he had not made himself popular with a lot of people. For instance, at the entrance gate to the property an "old witch" sat at her window in her little house the whole day and kept an eye on him. A couple of times she had already reported him to the police as a "German spy." But he also spoke of the girl's mother, whose employee he was, with scarcely concealed hostility; she really wanted to put her daughter into a convent. The man who at the beginning had been so taciturn had now had his tongue entirely loosened by the wine.

Meantime, midnight was approaching. He stood up with some difficulty, but he immediately dismissed any doubt about his fitness to drive. He was swaying slightly as the Doctor and I accompanied him to his car. We thanked him again, and he drove back to the farm "at a walking pace," as he called it.

After what had happened and what we had just heard, we were almost at a loss for words and, dead tired, we went to bed without further ado.

The next day, with renewed curiosity we walked around the truly amazing city of Poitiers, not at all prepared for such an array of superb architectural buildings. In this city of only fifty thousand inhabitants there were three churches, each big enough to serve as a cathedral. Two of them, Romanesque in style, bore the word "Grand" in their name; and where else in these northern latitudes would you find, in its original form, an early Christian baptistery dating from the fourth century.

It was strange how little we were inclined to speak about our adventure with the "chauvinist." But we were nearly finished with our usual midday snack taken in the open air off the main road when I began trying to reconstruct in some detail the strange chain of events of the previous day. The Doctor listened with some detachment and wound up the discussion with a comment that was as brief as it was unexpected: "Hopefully the girl's mother dies a natural death!" Then he lay back for his usual siesta and fell silent.

My wife, who was busy preparing the meal, had hardly said a word to all this. But when, after the rest period, at tea — which it was now her turn to prepare — it became clear that something had occurred to her which neither the Doctor nor I had thought of. "Your report has omitted something important. The 'old witch' really was sitting at the open window of her little house. And, by the way, she did not at all look like a witch. I noticed that she was watching us very intently." In fact, we men, sitting behind the windscreen, had not noticed the woman at all. But on this Sunday afternoon she did, indeed, get to see some highly unusual and very suspicious things. This extremely unlikeable German, this *boche* whom she had long since suspected of being a spy, had driven into the yard followed by a car with a West German registration number — on a day when there was no one else at home: the owners had gone away. After a short time the man drives off again in his car; the Germans remain in the yard; it is not clear what they are doing. An hour later the *boche* comes back. And again after a long delay the German car drives away, but this time it is closely followed by the *boche*'s car. Very late at night this man comes back alone, driving very slowly; naturally, he is drunk. She is used to seeing that. "And let us suppose," my wife said, "that the 'witch' has seen and made a note of the registration number of our car. That is quite feasible." Both men complimented our companion on her acumen as a criminalist. Apart from the last surmise, everything was completely realistic. Preoccupied with our thoughts we got into the car.

Then, when we were having our evening meal in Périgueux, to our surprise the Doctor took up the thread again. "Well, Madame, let us suppose that the witch not only made a note of our number but in fact also reported it to the police; this time she would really have something concrete to talk about. And, in any case, the German is a person already known to the police for a long time. In the meantime she is sure to know where our car is: namely, here in Périgueux. In the morning we could be greeted at breakfast by a police inspector and asked a few questions. The awkward part is that we would not be able to give one single plausible answer to any of the questions. That was clear. So: 'How did you come to know this man?' — 'We don't know this man; we don't even know his name.' 'Then how do you explain the fact that before you spoke to him he came out of the café in Chauvigny, approached your car, then paid his bill and immediately drove out with you to the farm where he lives. We have been informed of all of this.' Naturally we will tell the completely improbable story of the breakdown which no one who knows about cars would believe. 'Next: what did you speak about when you were with your acquaintance at the farm. You did know that, on that day, no one else was in the house?' — 'No, we didn't know that. We hardly conversed at all. The man was busy removing the tank. Then he took it to a friend who repaired it.' — 'And you are saying you have never seen the man and his friend before?' — 'That's right. We still have not seen his friend. We don't know him at all.' — 'Next: you spent the evening with the man?' — 'Yes, we had an evening meal together in Poitiers; that's what he wanted; he would not accept money.' – 'But you did talk to one another during the meal?' — 'Yes. He told us his story — or at least some of it. But he did not give us his name. We still don't know his name.' — 'Well, we are going to check out all of that. We will need your passports and car documents. In one or two days everything will be settled.' — This is the kind of thing we might have to deal with. And then in this French province, if this was all, we'd be getting off lightly." Naturally, all of that had not happened (as yet), but it was in no way an unrealistic thought.

In any case, the velvety red wine of the area could not guarantee us a peaceful night's sleep. We think we are making a bright summer's art excursion visiting Romanesque France and then, in our dreams we would be haunted by the terrifyingly hideous images of the figures we had photographed on the capitals. — Days later we were driving down into another entirely exotic world: that of the Lascaux caves.

Directly after this almost violent break, the unexpected onset of continual rain forced us to drive, in great haste, down south to the Pyrenees. Thus, in our secret thoughts, we thought also for a moment that the police were losing track of us. We had almost needed their help — when the Doctor, ignoring the travel guide warning, drove us up the spiraling unsealed road to the unique Prieuré de Serrabone, and down again. But in this secluded place there are no police far and wide. And fortunately, during the weeks of our journey home there was also no sign of them.

In any case, as we looked at the photos, what we had experienced twenty years ago seemed as unreal to us as a fairy story from time immemorial.

In manus tuas...

On Easter Sunday 1985 we could have celebrated our golden wedding anniversary. Our parish priest was willing to celebrate Mass on that occasion in our house at the table at which we had had our family meals until a few years ago — under the Rembrandt painting with the Emmaus disciples, which had been hanging there since our wedding day. In reality nobody really thought that we would reach that day. For about a year my wife could not have understood what we were talking about when the children and I spoke of this possibility. She died ten months before the anticipated date.

At first the problem was not too threatening. The fact that she could no longer keep the potter's wheel in motion with her foot was a blessing in disguise. Maria Martinez, the old Indian master craftswoman whom we had watched at work in New Mexico in 1956, had cast aside the electrical potter's wheel which the Washington Government had presented to her as a gift and was making her flawlessly symmetrical pots as surely as ever with her bare hands. And gradually the potter began to work in a similar way in our garden house, which had meantime become her workshop. This admittedly did not last for much longer than a decade; then all artistic activity ended. Happily we were able to go on many big trips during this period: Spain, Crete, Egypt, Morocco and finally Mexico and Guatemala. In these two latter countries we were, of course, particularly fascinated by the amazing buildings of the Aztecs and the Mayas; and we did not leave out many of them. The potter naturally wanted to see as much as possible in person;

and often enough I saw her climbing around the almost forbidding monuments with her walking stick, both amazed and fearful all at once; but clearly the stimulating mountain air of the Mexican high planes made her forget her pain and her disability. On the last trip abroad — to Portugal, in the late summer of 1969 — she had to rely on a rental car driven by our daughter Monika, who had to bring her as near as possible to the Algarve beach, where she then lay on her stomach on the warm sand and read; or she watched with ungrudging enjoyment while her husband and daughter played ball.

But at that time the operation had already been decided on: during the following spring she was to have an artificial hip inserted in Munich University Hospital. She did not fear this dangerous procedure at all. And as it turned out that the procedure was to go ahead on our thirty-fifth wedding anniversary, I got the feeling, from her buoyant and hugely hopeful letter full of impatient expectation, that the date was a good omen. And then when I arrived in Munich ten days later at the semester break, the nicest birthday present of my life awaited me: my sweet wife stepped towards me fully dressed. She was still somewhat uncertain on her feet, but hardly needed any support at all. It was a real celebration; and we spoke excitedly about the new phase of life which was about to begin. But unfortunately the period of joy was very short.

It would be pointless to outline the unexpected afflictions which followed, in an unending chain, one after the other. And there was no shortage of medical misdiagnoses, failed operations, or wrong therapies. In any case neither the distant rheumatism hospital nor the rural hospital which specialized in gymnastic exercise, massage and "rehabilitation," nor the orthopedic and finally even the neurological University hospital brought any real help. And so several times there was a period of hopes being aroused, which then ended in disappointment, followed by a long period of suffering, which ultimately ended in death.

That sounds completely dismal, and it really was a bad and sad time. However, that is not all there is to say on the matter and also not the most crucial part. During the first weeks when my wife realized to her alarm that she had unwittingly ended up in a prison cell from which there was no escape, it must have been for her a time of paralyzing fear and deep consternation. Her loud cries for help in words she normally did not use (Mercy!) sounded gruesomely through the house as a bitter complaint. But after a while all of a sudden these cries for help stopped. And it seemed that there was a change in the soul of the person who realized that she was seriously ill — whereby no one understood what produced the change nor understood exactly what it meant. But it looks as if she decided, in a moment, not to cast off the serenity of her soul. At this time she may have secretly, in the loneliness of the hospital wards, learned some psalms and hymns off by heart from the precious "Instruments of Daily Prayers" which we had received as a present from my publisher friend Heinrich Wild. Although she was not well versed in Latin, there was among them the *Adoro Te,* which she later recited or rather prayed many times: the Eucharistic hymn of Thomas Aquinas. Our son Michael — to whom she occasionally spoke about her death while she studiously avoided ever speaking to me about it — asked her once what she thought about death. She replied: "Some particular words from the bible come into my mind." However, she did not tell him which words they were. After Michael had written to me in a letter about this I asked my wife, and the somewhat hesitant answer came: "For example: I have called you by your name: you are mine!"

By her own personal efforts she managed, despite some recurring setbacks, to avoid sinking into the depths of misery during those bad years. I'm convinced that there was also another important factor in this. Apart from the fact that we had exceptionally good, selfless and encouraging helpers, there was an even more telling factor which was completely taken for granted, and about which there was no discussion between us, not even a word. Again and again I was given the well-intentioned advice that I should entrust her to the care of a "home" which was much better equipped to look after her. However, I never once gave this any consideration; and my wife knew this very well. We simply wanted to stay together "during the good times as well as the bad," though spending some periods in hospital had been unavoidable. She rightly only felt "at home" in the house which we had occupied together for more than forty years, and in her garden which she had looked after with love and expertise.

Here, too, she gradually regained her natural vital energy which had often amazed us. Once, for example, she spent days in intensive care in the University Clinic after a heavy fall down the stone steps of the cellar — probably caused by a brain hemorrhage. The young chaplain at the clinic had immediately performed the last rites on her, something which I only found out later. I informed my son and daughter as a precautionary measure. The young female doctor who was looking after her let me know in no uncertain terms that it did not look good. But then when Michael, who had traveled overnight from Munich, came to his mother's bed and she was almost unrecognizable because of the apparatus for artificial feeding and for the intravenous drip, she opened her eyes and said in a clear voice: "What happiness to see you!" The crisis had been averted; a few hours later she was sleeping soundly in her own ward; and not long after that — though it was still a matter of weeks — she was allowed to return home. During this time the older chaplain at the clinic informed me, a little surprised but at the same time showing deep respect, that my wife had once pushed his hand which contained the sacred host gently to one side and recited, before receiving communion, the whole seven verses of *Adoro te;* he was embarrassed that he did not know it off by heart, but he had in the meantime learned it.

At home, our customary reading aloud was no longer possible.

Before the last operation — it was the sixth — she had rightly said: "Another anaesthetic? I won't survive that!" And actually we had to break off our shared reading in the middle of Golo Mann's "Wallenstein"; she was no longer able to follow the sophisticated text. But still we had the consolation of music. The last Beethoven Quartets, a Bach chorale played by Dinu Lipatti, and particularly Bruckner's *Te Deum,* which she listened to in a quite new receptive way, only now opened to her all their enchanting strength. It was also a pleasure, during our almost daily walks with the wheelchair through what my wife called the "quiet streets," for us to remember the events we had shared during our trips and early adventures. What was surprising was to experience that we were able to speak about things which, had we been speaking face to face, would have been left unsaid. Of course, the gardener could not resist kneeling on her trusted oil cloth cushion in order to tidy up the garden; naturally she had to be helped down and up again, which certainly could not have been done without her experiencing pain; still it was clear that she was really happy for a period. Many times on seeing her blooming lilies she repeated with delight the biblical words: "Not even Solomon in all his glory was dressed as one of these!"

One afternoon she wanted me to sit beside her because she wanted to say something important; she was speaking with unusual seriousness. And then she put her arm around my shoulder and said something which I will never forget. But first you must know a story which only later became clear to me. Presumably she could not forget a conversation she had had almost a decade ago with the wife of my brother who had died quite unexpectedly. She regretted, and also found surprising, that her husband had died without any goodbyes. At the time, I had listened to the women and said that when one is confronted so suddenly with the possibility of one's impending death one is understandably totally preoccupied and there is no place for any other thought. Clearly she did not want it to reach this point; she would not want to miss this moment for anything. She felt that she herself was going downhill and she feared that one day perhaps she would not be able to think and speak clearly any longer. So she probably was thinking of that conversation when she put her arm around my shoulder and said a single wonderful sentence for no one's ear but mine. But although it was whispered, it sounded like an oath. But then we drank our tea and listened to music as usual.

She was able to think and speak clearly for a while after that. But we had to give up the trips in the wheelchair, including those to the Saturday evening Mass. The priest brought her Communion every Sunday morning. And while we prepared a little for it together I gradually learned what an amazing number of prayers she had committed to memory — the Latin Pentecost Sequence, for example, several psalms, and a long prayer from the "Teachings of the Twelve Apostles" which I did not know myself and which began with the words: "We give thanks to thee Our Father for thy holy name, thou who hast come to dwell in our hearts." She had already partly forgotten some of these texts, even the *Adoro Te; we* still tried at first to keep the hymns in mind through playful memory exercises: "*O memoriale mortis Domini* – how does it go?" But then that did not work either. The last prayer which she still recited clearly before the priest came was again in Latin with a small grammatical error: *In manus tuas, Domine, commendo spiritus meum.* She had never said anything confused, even later, but more and more what she wanted to express slipped from her mental and linguistic grasp. However, the strong hand of the potter and gardener could still take hold of things with unexpected power, and whatever she took hold of she often did not want to let go of again. Then for more than a year spoken conversation was finally completely at an end. Of course, the communication between us never ended, even if it was confined to physical touching, or a friendly groaning and humming; I am convinced that she could see me and look at me through her eyelids, which were almost always closed. It is not possible to guess what was going on in her head and what might have moved her in her heart of hearts. Sometimes at the beginning of a sentence ("We should someday ...") you thought that you could understand a tiny bit; but then it disappeared again immediately.

On Monday of the week of Corpus Christi, before I travelled to Cologne for a reading from the first chapters of this as yet unpublished autobiography, I decided to take a photograph of my wife as she sat seemingly asleep in her armchair, with her bony craftworker's hands on the tartan blanket covering her knees. I did not yet know that it was to be the last day of her life that she would sit in this armchair the way she had done for a few years. When I got home around midnight a decision had been taken which I did not yet know about. The doctor believed that she could not stand for outpatient care for her because of a sudden, at first puzzling, presumably cancerous deterioration in her illness. So the following morning the Caritas Sisters arrived and washed the patient in the usual way and freshened her up. They did not dress her but brought her back to bed. The room in the hospital to which she was to be brought would be available at midday. And so she finally had to leave our house and her "home" six days before her death.

Although I had seen two people die, my younger brother and a short time later my mother, I had not yet witnessed what we nowadays call, downplaying it somewhat, "the anointing of the sick" —not even at the anointing which had been bestowed on my wife on one occasion already. But when on the morning of Corpus Christi I was coming from the Pontifical Mass in the Cathedral and I saw the priest enter the ward almost at the same time as I did, I knew that what was going to take place was the once and still validly named liturgical *extrema unctio,* "the last anointment," the sacrament of the dying. What amazed me most was the skill with which the ceremonious action was carried out, with the accompanying established formulae, simply ignoring the technical instruments which had almost made the patient unrecognizable. Her forehead was still free; and I myself held up both her hands for anointing. It was completely obvious: what was happening here was not pious consolation but plainly sacramental reality.

On the afternoon of the day she died, when I returned to the hospital with my son and daughter, they had removed the drip feed and infusion apparatus; there was no longer any use for them. The doctor judged that she had about seven to eight hours to live. Our mother, as I also had called her for years, lay there quite peacefully; but her face had surprisingly changed; it looked like that of a young girl. I do not know and I rather doubt if my children noticed it too. I saw it anyway — and I was at once charmed and startled. What had happened in the meantime to this tired, old woman of whom I had taken a photograph only a few days ago? She was hardly recognizable! Who can say, I thought, what she had to go through in these few days and nights, what unfathomable inner experiences had been produced in her, shaken her into bright awareness and haunted her? But she seemed to have left this behind her, and her so unexpectedly young-looking face was like that of a young runner who was a little exhausted, but radiant with a trace of triumphal cheerfulness because of having survived.

By evening the face had changed again; it appeared to have become smaller and to be expressing a childish defenselessness, but at the same time something like happiness at not having to struggle any longer. Her arms lay outstretched on the blanket. I sat down beside her and held her right hand which had long since let go of everything which needed to be held; her hand lay open and flat in mine. There was not the least doubt in my mind that we were constantly looking at one another, although her eyes were closed. – At my request Michael read the psalm his mother loved so much "The Lord is my light and my salvation," which includes the wonderful verse: "On the day of doom he protects me." There was otherwise hardly a word spoken. We felt blessed that all three of us, and just the three of us, could be with her during these hours and until the end. How often had I thought during my trips in recent times: please do not let her die when I am away.

Near midnight her breathing became noticeably shallow and, though calm, shorter and shorter — until the last breath came. I stood up, placed my hand around her neck and said with my face very close to her: "Mother, now we can say: *'In manus tuas ...'*," and I repeated her own last prayer including the grammatical error. — I am certain that in this mysterious, timeless moment of passing over from earthly life she did not just hear it but also prayed it with me.